JUN 24 1991

DEMCO

ZOO ANIMALS

BY

DONALD F. HOFFMEISTER
Director, Natural History Museum
and Professor of Zoology, University of Illinois

Under the editorship of

HERBERT S. ZIM and GEORGE S. FICHTER

Illustrated by

ARTHUR SINGER

Young
Asian
Elephant

A GOLDEN NATURE GUIDE

 GOLDEN PRESS • NEW YORK
Western Publishing Company, Inc.
Racine, Wisconsin

FOREWORD

In the mid-1960's, the world had at least 440 zoos—including about 120 in the U.S. and 175 in Europe. New zoos are being built, and in total they attract many millions of visitors annually.

Thanks are due many individuals for their aid in preparing this book. James H. Amon, Ronald Blakely, Roger Conant, Lee Crandall, Gene Hartz, Harry Henriksen, S. C. Kendeigh, Ray Pawley, George Pournelle, Henry Saunders, and Hobart M. Smith were especially helpful. Special thanks are due Arthur Singer for his excellent illustrations.

D.F.H.

PHOTO CREDITS:
Bethlehem Steel, 102; Brookfield Zoo, Chicago, 6 (bottom), 12 (bottom), 13 (top right); Bullerman, Milwaukee County Zoo, 9 (top), 13 (bottom right); George S. Fichter, 6 (middle), 12 (top); Lincoln Park Zoo, Chicago, 6 (top); Monkmeyer Press Photo Service, 5 (bottom); Arthur Singer, 9 (bottom), 13 (bottom left); Fred J. Zeehandelaar, 5 (top); H. S. Zim, 13 (top left).

CONTENTS

Quetzal
body 14 in.;
tail 24 in.

INTRODUCING ZOOS

Zoos are maintained for the education and enjoyment of visitors and for scientific work with animals. Many of the animals are from parts of the world where the visitors are not likely to travel. Zoos exhibit such well-known animals as lions, bears, and monkeys; many also include interesting local animals. In modern zoos, animals are kept in habitat settings that are as nearly natural as possible. Zoos serve an important function as sanctuaries for rare, wild animals.

Working behind the scenes in most zoos are zoologists, veterinarians, medical doctors, and other scientists. They study breeding and reproduction, nutrition, physiology, behavior, diseases, and special housing.

WILD ANIMALS have probably been kept in captivity through all history. The oldest zoos on record were in Egypt in 1400 B.C. and China in 1100 B.C. The large collections of the Romans included lions, tigers, and other ferocious beasts that were pitted against gladiators. Many early rulers kept private menageries of interesting or unusual animals—mainly for personal enjoyment. Public zoos were established in Paris, France, in 1793. Oldest in the U.S., the Philadelphia Zoo, was started in 1859, opened in 1874. Zoos in Peking, China, Bronx, N.Y., and San Diego, Calif. are among largest. Nearly all big cities now have zoos.

From quarantine corral in Kenya, crated giraffes travel to N.Y.

ZOO ANIMALS are obtained in a variety of ways. A century ago, expeditions to far-off places were common. These have been largely replaced by purchases from professional collectors and by exchanges, trades, or purchases from other zoos, or from foreign wildlife and game departments. Professional animal dealers are skilled at capturing animals safely and in caring for them properly during the quarantine period before they are shipped. They know how to condition animals to their new diet in captivity and how to ship them, often by air, for safe arrival.

There are many ways to capture animals. Birds and porpoises are netted. Some birds can be caught by using a long pole with a sticky material at the tip to entangle them. A solvent removes the sticky substance from the feathers. Traps, snares, and corrals are used to capture mammals. Special guns that shoot a non-lethal dose of a tranquilizing or paralyzing drug are the most effective and also the most humane method used today.

Many zoo animals are born in captivity. These zoo-reared animals represent generations that have known no life in the wild.

Seals are shipped by air from one zoo to another.

Baby Macaque is spoon fed in nursery.

Rejected "joey" is reared in zoo.

ANIMALS BORN IN THE ZOO are given special care. They are important in maintaining the displays and are special attractions while they are young. The growth rates of these zoo babies are checked and recorded regularly by the zoo veterinarians.

Many animals will not breed in captivity; others will do so only under controlled conditions or diets. Pens are often provided for expectant females. If the mother does not care for her young or rejects them, the infants may be removed. Many newborn animals, especially those of some of the primates and cats, are placed in incubators much like those used in hospitals. Others are put in a nursery where the temperature and humidity are controlled. They are watched carefully and are fed special diets.

Formulas for infant animals in the zoo nurseries include powdered or evaporated milk, sugar syrup, multiple-vitamins, and antibiotics. The young must be fed at frequent intervals night and day. As the baby animal grows, its formula is gradually changed until finally it is able to eat adult foods.

Birds in a zoo may mate, nest, then lay eggs and hatch them. If fertile eggs are neglected, some may be hatched in incubators. Eggs of snakes, turtles, and lizards may also be hatched in incubators in which the humidity is kept high.

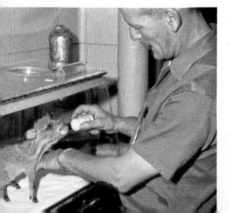

Newborn Collared Peccary is fed by bottle while still in the incubator.

ZOOS CONSERVE RARE ANIMALS, and some kinds live today only because they have been preserved in breeding groups. Among these animals are Père David's Deer, Wisent, Arabian Oryx, White-tailed Gnu, Blesbok, and Przewalski's Horse. Other animals that are nearly extinct in their native lands may be saved if zoos are successful in breeding them. The Gorilla, Pigmy Hippo, various lemurs, White and Indian rhinoceroses, the Galapagos Tortoise, Whooping Crane, Trumpeter Swan, and Néné are among species in danger of extinction as their natural environments are being destroyed. To assure their survival, zoos develop special areas where these animals can breed and rear offspring. On the list of rare and endangered animals that need protection are several hundred species.

Néné

Trumpeter Swan

Arabian Oryx

Wisent

White-tailed Gnu

DISPLAYS in modern zoos create as nearly as possible the natural environment in which an animal or group of animals is found. In some displays, the animals appear to be living together but are actually separated by moats or by concealed fences. Many animals, however, are compatible and can be kept safely in the same enclosure. These include such African waterhole species as zebras, ostriches, and elands; emus, wallabies, and kangaroos from the Australian plains; rheas, guanacos, and cavies from the South American plains. Groups of monkeys, usually baboons or macaques and sometimes other primates, are commonly kept on a rocky island in a pond large enough to prevent their escape. Males often fight, and it may be necessary to remove all but one to keep peace.

Flight cages for birds may be indoors or outdoors but are large enough for trees and for pools of water. In them, birds can fly, court, nest, and rear their young.

Small delicate animals are usually kept in special buildings in which the temperature, humidity, and light can be controlled. Here desert animals can be exhibited in the coldest weather or penguins when it is hottest.

In many zoos, moats separate people and animals. For each kind of animal the depth and width of the moat is specific, depending on the animal's ability to jump. The moat may be dry or filled with water. Shown here are three kinds of moats for different kinds of animals.

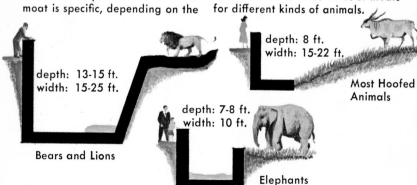

depth: 13-15 ft.
width: 15-25 ft.

Bears and Lions

depth: 8 ft.
width: 15-22 ft.

Most Hoofed Animals

depth: 7-8 ft.
width: 10 ft.

Elephants and Rhinos

Elephants, rhinos, and other Asian animals share same zoo exhibit.

Polar Bears and Stellar Sea Lions occupy adjoining spaces.

Some hummingbirds and many amphibians and reptiles require air-conditioned quarters. Aquatic animals, such as penguins and seals, are displayed most effectively with viewing areas above and below surface of water.

Penguins swim in Bronx Zoo's enclosed, air-conditioned pool.

Fennec Fox and other nocturnals are displayed in dim red lights.

FOODS AND DIETS of zoo animals are so varied that a zoo's "kitchen" must be well stocked. Staples include fresh fruits, vegetables, grains, hay, bean and nut oils, sunflower seeds, horse meat, and milk, plus the vitamins and minerals added to nearly all diets. Without adequate and balanced diets (some must be accurately proportioned and weighed), zoo animals will neither thrive nor breed and also become susceptible to diseases.

HERBIVORES

also fed concentrates of grains, soybean oil, salt, vitamins, often as pellets

hay

salt

grain or meal

CARNIVORES

raw meat, with vitamins and minerals

small mammals for birds of prey and snakes

horse meat for larger carnivores

SPECIAL DIETS

seal

penguin

lizard

frog

flamin

ibis

SPECIAL DIETS must be provided for many zoo animals.

Among the animals requiring special diets (below) are the seals and penguins that need fish. Lizards and frogs require mealworms, crickets, roaches, or other live insects. Flamingos, Scarlet Ibises, and other birds with bright plumage may be kept in good color if their diets include carrots, beets, or other foods rich in red and yellow pigments (carotenoids). Anteaters are fed a soupy mix of hard-boiled eggs, milk, and cooked meat; hummingbirds, a honey or sugar syrup; lorikeets, a sweetened porridge. Koalas require eucalyptus tree leaves.

MANY CAGED BIRDS

boiled eggs

fruit

vitamins and minerals added

seeds and grains

meal

cooked meat

OMNIVORES

fruit

"cake mix" of meal, grain, vitamins, dry meat

milk

greens

giant anteater

lorikeet

hummer

koala

A meerkat, cut in fight with cage companions, is anesthetized while the wound is cleaned and treated by veterinarian at Crandon Park Zoo, Miami.

MEDICAL CARE of sick or injured animals is provided in the zoo's hospital, where veterinarians perform operations, set bones, and cure diseases. These specialists in animal medicine use the latest drugs and equipment.

Newly acquired animals are held in isolation rooms until it can be determined that they are free of disease and parasites. Recovery areas give sick animals a quiet place to regain health.

Minor but essential procedures include trimming nails, claws, and hoofs; removal of antlers; and repair and extraction of teeth. Animals were once held quiet in squeeze cages. Nearly all zoos now use tranquilizer drugs that can be injected from a distance with a gun. In this way even the largest and most dangerous animals can be given medical attention without danger to animals or attendants.

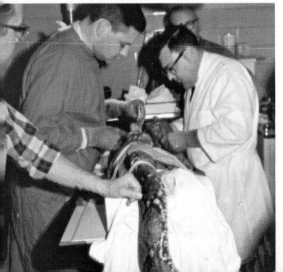

Veterinarians and members of staff at Chicago's Brookfield Zoo operate on an anesthetized Reticulated Python, to remove a tumor from its stomach region.

Children are treated to a ride in a decorated goat cart at the zoo in Mexico City.

At the zoo in Mexico City, trained Indian Elephants perform stunts daily for visitors.

CHILDREN'S ZOOS are one of the most important parts of most zoos. In these specially designed areas, young people can approach and even handle many animals, both wild and domestic. Here they can see sheep, chickens, ducks, geese, pigs, ponies, and other farm animals, too. They can watch cows being milked, sheep shorn, and eggs hatching. With a keeper's guidance, children may also handle baby lions, monkeys, parrots, raccoons, and other animals. A ride on a giant tortoise is always a thrill.

Some zoos have "shows," including trained animal acts. The feeding of such animals as sea lions, the large cats, and some kinds of birds is an interesting show in itself. Some animals put on performances of their own. Bears will clown, and monkeys will caper to attract attention.

Ducks and geese live in an open pond almost within reach at Bronx Zoo. Children feed them.

An Alaskan Brown Bear clowns soberly for an audience at the Milwaukee County Zoo.

Platypus

MAMMALS

Mammals are the only furred animals. They have mammary glands to provide milk for their young, which are air-breathing and active when born. Specialized teeth of several types are set in sockets in the upper and lower jaws. The 15,000 species are diverse in size, appearance, and habits. Of those kept in zoos, many require special diets and controlled conditions.

MONOTREMES, the most primitive mammals, lay eggs and have mammary glands without teats. The milk is secreted onto areas of the skin and hair. Echidnas and the Platypus live only in the Australian region.

ECHIDNAS, or Spiny Anteaters (1–2 ft. long), are covered with spines. Toothless, they use their sticky tongues to entangle termites and ants. In captivity they eat ground meat, chopped eggs and milk. A single egg is incubated in female's pouch where newborn remains until too large.

PLATYPUSES, seldom seen but not uncommon in their native Australia, are rare in zoos because of export restrictions. They have a ducklike bill, swim with webbed feet, and lay 1 or 2 eggs in underground nest. Males 2 ft. long, weigh 3 lbs. In zoos, eat worms, shrimp, insects.

Echidna

MARSUPIALS, of the Australian region, South America, and a few in North America, are mammals in which the young, very immature at birth, continue to grow and nurse in the female's abdominal pouch.

WOMBATS (36 in.) are heavy-bodied, short-tailed, burrowing marsupials of Australia. They feed on grass, hay, roots, vegetables, and bark. Nocturnal burrowers, hence display poorly.

TASMANIAN DEVILS (26 in.), found now only on the island of Tasmania, feed on small mammals, frogs, birds. Pouch opens to rear, as in some other marsupials and unlike kangaroos.

Tasmanian Devil

Wombat

Koala

KOALAS (28 in.; under 30 lbs.) are Australian marsupials that feed on the oily, tough leaves of eucalyptus trees in which they live. The single young lives for 2 months in the mother's pouch, later clings to her back. Nearly extinct, Koalas are found in only two zoos outside Australia.

Red Kangaroo

Great Gray Kangaroo

female with "joey"

KANGAROOS AND WALLABIES are long-footed, jumping marsupials of Australia and New Guinea. The largest kangaroo, the Great Gray, measures over 7 ft. and weighs 200 lbs. Wallabies are smaller kangaroos, some no larger than rabbits. Some of the heavy-bodied kangaroos are called wallaroos. Kangaroos of all kinds have short front legs, long hind legs, and a thick, round tail that provides support when sitting and a balance when jumping. In zoos, kangaroos may be fed mink and monkey chow, hay, vegetables, even fruit. They frequently breed and rear young in captivity. The young, usually one, weighs 1 oz. at birth, lives in pouch until it grows too large to get in.

Brush-tailed
Rock Wallaby

Ring-tailed
Rock Wallaby

Red-necked
Wallaby

RED KANGAROOS, nearly as large as Great Grays, are excellent jumpers, traveling for miles with leaps of 10 ft. or more and at speeds up to 25 miles an hour. Males are usually red, females, bluish gray. Reds and Great Grays frequently live together in groups called "mobs."

ROCK WALLABIES are small-bodied, 18–28 in. The padded soles and stiff hairs on their hind feet prevent the animals from slipping on rocks. They eat grasses, leaves, and bark. The Brush-tailed and Ring-tailed are two of the several species.

GREAT GRAY KANGAROOS (7 ft.; 200 lbs.) are sometimes called Foresters, for they live in the grasslands of the open forests of Australia. Males, larger than females, are "boomers"; the young, "joeys." When too large to get into the pouch, a joey inserts its head to nurse.

RED-NECKED WALLABIES are medium-sized—body about 30 in.; tail, 27 in. They prefer brush country and, unlike the Red and Great Gray kangaroos, rarely venture into open grasslands. In almost all the shoulders are reddish brown.

Wallaroo

Tree Kangaroo

TREE KANGAROOS (26 in.) hop into trees to feed on leaves. They use their long hands for grasping branches, their tail as a prop. During the day, they usually sleep or hide in trees.

WALLAROOS, also called Rock Kangaroos, prefer gullies and steep slopes of rocky country. Several kinds (to 5 ft. tall) are widely distributed in Australia. In captivity, males may fight.

AMERICAN OPOSSUMS (18 in.) have a long, scaly tail, leaflike ears, and grasping feet. They feed on plant or animal matter, living or dead. To avoid enemies, they run, hide, or play dead.

MOUSE OPOSSUMS, about the size of large mice, are found from Mexico to South America. They eat insects and fruit; in captivity, dog food and milk. Females lack pouches.

American Opossum

Mouse Opossum

PLACENTALS are mammals in which the unborn young, more developed than in monotremes and marsupials, are nourished directly by the mother through a special tissue, the placenta.

PRIMATES have a well-developed brain, eyes directed forward, and, in most, flattened nails on fingers and toes. Included are apes, monkeys, lemurs, tree shrews, and tarsiers. The manlike apes have long arms, short legs, no tail, and no cheek pounches.

GORILLAS are the largest of the apes. Males may stand over 5 ft. tall and weigh more than 500 lbs.; females are smaller. Mountain-dwelling gorillas of Central Africa have black coats; lowland, or coastal, gorillas are rusty gray. In captivity, an adult eats 30 to 40 lbs. of fruit, vegetables, and meat a day.

Coastal Gorilla

male

female

ORANGUTANS are stockily built apes from tropical forests of Borneo and Sumatra. Males weigh about 200 lbs. and may develop flabby cheek pads and throat sacs. Orangs avoid walking. With an arm spread of nearly 8 ft., they swing gracefully through the trees in which they build nestlike homes. In captivity, orangs are deliberate, often inactive. Old orangs (30+ yrs.) may be mean.

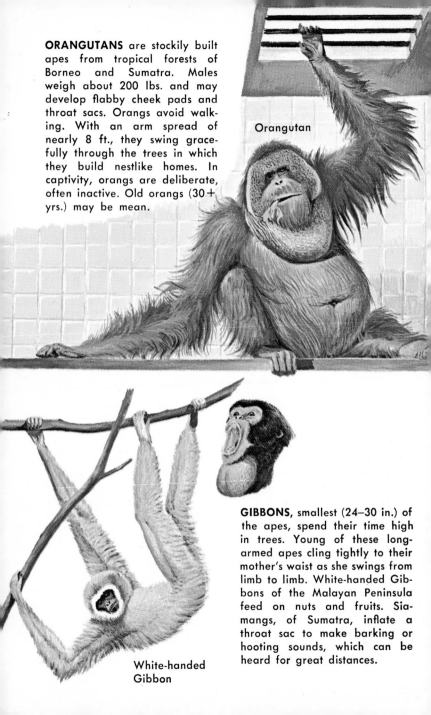

Orangutan

GIBBONS, smallest (24–30 in.) of the apes, spend their time high in trees. Young of these long-armed apes cling tightly to their mother's waist as she swings from limb to limb. White-handed Gibbons of the Malayan Peninsula feed on nuts and fruits. Siamangs, of Sumatra, inflate a throat sac to make barking or hooting sounds, which can be heard for great distances.

White-handed Gibbon

CHIMPANZEES, or Chimps, are tree dwellers from tropical Africa. They weigh 130 to 140 lbs. (rarely to 190). Chimps can stand erect (5 ft.), but they prefer to walk on all fours, using the knuckles on their hands. Their arms extend below their knees even when the animals are standing straight.

Chimps are good showmen in zoos. They enjoy applause, which they may start themselves when they have finished a performance. Chimps also have temper tantrums. Because of their high intelligence, chimps have been studied intensively. In their early life they seem to learn and develop faster than humans. They master simple skills quickly and also show some ability to reason.

Both in the wild and in zoos, chimps are highly sociable. Adults are often dangerous. Like all primates, they should have warm, dry cages with high humidity. Chimps relish a variety of fruits (apples, bananas, grapes, oranges), vegetables (carrots, lettuce, celery, potatoes), and cooked meats. Their diet is not much different from that of Orangs and Gorillas.

male

female

Chimpanzee

OLD WORLD MONKEYS include macaques, some so-called apes, baboons, languars, and other monkeys of Africa, Asia, and India. Many are tail-less; if they have a tail, it is not prehensile (grasping). The nostrils are close together and directed downward, most species have callosities on the buttocks, many have cheek pouches, and all have only 32 teeth. Barbary Apes and some other larger species are kept outdoors in warm months; others are housed in glass-fronted cages to prevent them from acquiring human-borne diseases and to avoid disrupting their normal habits.

CELEBES CRESTED APES, or Black Apes (22 in.), are not true apes but closely related to the macaques. When excited, they erect a tuft of hair on top of the head. Like macaques, they have a knoblike tail and a long, straight nose. They are native to Island of Celebes.

BARBARY APE, or Magot (30 in.), a species of macaque, lives along the Barbary Coast of Africa and on Gibraltar. In captivity as in the wild, they stay in large groups. Captives stare at visitors. Some develop the bad habit of throwing stones and splashing water.

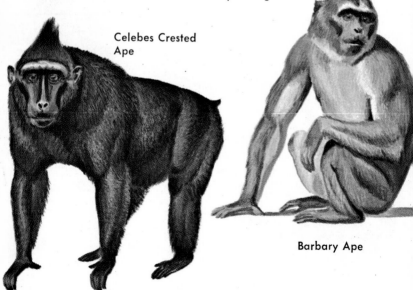

Celebes Crested Ape

Barbary Ape

Brown Stump-tailed Macaque

Rhesus Monkey

Javan Macaque

Pig-tailed Macaque

STUMPED-TAIL MACAQUES (several species) all have very short tails. The 30 in. Brown Stumptail of Southeast Asia has a red face. Young are cradled in the arms, somewhat hidden by fur.

RHESUS MONKEYS (22 in.) are macaques that roam in large, noisy, semiorganized troops from India to China and Formosa. They do well in captivity: breed, eat nearly anything, withstand cold. Rhesus monkeys are used extensively in medical research.

JAVAN MACAQUES are small (20 in.), easily tamed but mischievous, even destructive. Like most macaques, they usually become mean with age. Longer tailed than most macaques.

PIG-TAILED MACAQUES (20 in.) carry their thin tail erect or sometimes curled. Groups live in dense lowland forests of Southeast Asia. Sometimes trained to harvest coconuts.

OLD WORLD MONKEYS—MACAQUES 23

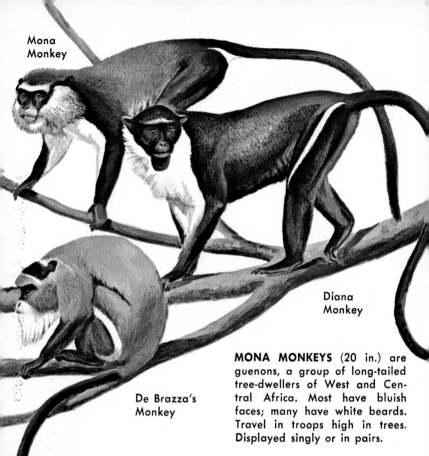

Mona Monkey

Diana Monkey

De Brazza's Monkey

MONA MONKEYS (20 in.) are guenons, a group of long-tailed tree-dwellers of West and Central Africa. Most have bluish faces; many have white beards. Travel in troops high in trees. Displayed singly or in pairs.

DE BRAZZA'S MONKEYS (24 in.) are bright-colored guenons with prominent goatee. De Brazza's Monkeys are strong jumpers, and they use their long tail as a balancing organ.

DIANA MONKEYS (18 in.) are "white-bibbed" guenons; they have a white goatee. Dianas live in trees and hide in the foliage. Like all guenons, they make a variety of sounds, and caged adults may become mean, especially if not given proper care.

Green Guenon

GREEN GUENONS, or Vervets (22 in.), similar to Monas, do well in captivity. They are active, agile, and ideal showmen. In parts of East Africa, Vervets are common in city parks.

MUSTACHED MONKEYS (23 in.) have mustache-like markings on the upper lip. These guenons are sometimes called Blue-faced Monkeys. Cheek beards are especially long. They travel in groups feeding on fruits, leaves, and small animals. This West African species lives in treetops in tropical forests. Captives do well.

SPOT-NOSED MONKEYS (20 in.) are distinguished by the white spot on the nose and the lack of a beard. They live in the treetops of dense jungles from the Congo to Liberia. They eat the leaves, flowers, and fruits of the trees in which they live.

PATAS MONKEYS (30 in.) are reddish with a hairy face and whitish chin whiskers. Unlike most other guenons, Patas are principally ground dwellers and run doglike across the grassy plains of north-central Africa. Their habit of jumping up and down resulted in the name Dancing Monkeys. Others thought their red-colored coats resembled those of the Hussars.

Mustached
Monkey

Spot-nosed
Monkey

Patas
Monkey

Javan Langur

Black and White Guereza

JAVAN LANGURS (24 in.) have a long, straight tail and a short nose. All langurs, which live in southern Asia, are excellent climbers and are leaf-eaters. In zoos, their diet may include soft leafy vegetables and fruits. Captives are generally, but not always, inactive, and they are usually short-lived. Cages must be large enough to give them space for leaps of 20 feet or more.

BLACK AND WHITE GUEREZAS, or Colobus (24 in.), are leaf-eating monkeys of Africa. This colorful monkey is black, with a white facial whorl, white mantle, and a white tasseled tail. The young are completely buffy-white. Guerezas move through the treetops with agility and are excellent jumpers. They are slower and more awkward on the ground. Guerezas are large monkeys, some males weighing more than 20 lbs. In captivity, these monkeys usually live only about 1 year, though one has survived more than 20 years. Like most other monkeys, the zoo diet consists of fruits and vegetables; meats are refused.

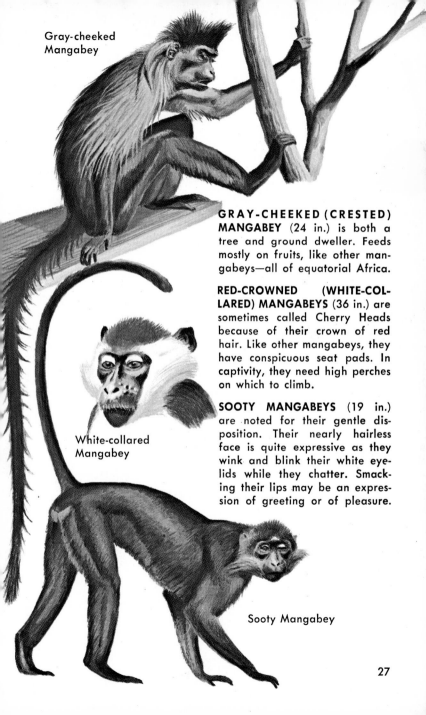

Gray-cheeked Mangabey

White-collared Mangabey

Sooty Mangabey

GRAY-CHEEKED (CRESTED) MANGABEY (24 in.) is both a tree and ground dweller. Feeds mostly on fruits, like other mangabeys—all of equatorial Africa.

RED-CROWNED (WHITE-COLLARED) MANGABEYS (36 in.) are sometimes called Cherry Heads because of their crown of red hair. Like other mangabeys, they have conspicuous seat pads. In captivity, they need high perches on which to climb.

SOOTY MANGABEYS (19 in.) are noted for their gentle disposition. Their nearly hairless face is quite expressive as they wink and blink their white eyelids while they chatter. Smacking their lips may be an expression of greeting or of pleasure.

27

CHACMA BABOONS (34 in.) live in the rocky country of South Africa. Other species live elsewhere in Africa and northward into Arabia. All of these muzzle-faced monkeys are mainly ground dwellers, running on all fours and traveling in well-organized troops. Drills and mandrills are baboons also. Chacmas are usually displayed in barred or moated cages. Some captives throw objects at visitors. Baboons are hardy and breed and rear young in captivity.

GELADA BABOONS (24 in.) have long manes, distinctively up-turned muzzles with the nostrils on the flat upper surface, a conspicuous red chest, and white eyelids. Males are much larger than the females.

HAMADRYAS BABOONS (28 in.) are the "sacred baboons" of ancient Egypt and are often pictured in early temples. Males, in contrast to females and young, have a heavy mane. All can make loud, doglike barks.

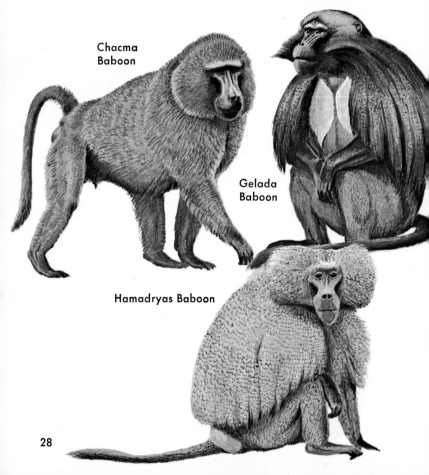

Chacma Baboon

Gelada Baboon

Hamadryas Baboon

28

DRILLS (26 in.), almost tail-less, live in the forests of the Cameroons in West Africa. Slightly smaller and less colorful than the closely related Mandrill, they occasionally climb trees and sleep there at night. The colorful rear patches of males are used in attracting mates. Like their long-tailed relatives, Drills usually travel in troops, often consisting of as many as 50 animals. Their growls and barks are a means of communication. Both the Drill and the Mandrill have lived to an age of more than 20 years (one reportedly to 46 years) in captivity.

Mandrill

Drill

MANDRILLS (29 in.) are the most bizarre of all mammals. No other mammal has a face as brightly colored as the male Mandrill's. Deep furrows line the long snout. The head is large, the tail stubby. Females are less brightly colored. Mandrills usually travel in small groups. They live mainly in the forests but may at times travel far into the open country to find their food. In captivity, the diet of both the Mandrill and the Drill is much the same as that for other baboons: fruits and vegetables, which are supplemented with meats to take the place of the small birds and mammals that they eat in the wild.

NEW WORLD MONKEYS are tree dwellers of the tropics of South and Central America and Mexico. In contrast to Old World monkeys, their nostrils are more separated and open to the sides rather than downward. They lack cheek pouches and callus pads on the buttocks, and many have a long prehensile tail. Except for marmosets, they have a full set of 36 teeth. In general, they do less well in zoos.

Woolly
Monkey

WOOLLY MONKEYS, of the Amazon Basin, have "crew haircuts" and woolly fur. Their tail is slightly longer than their 25-in. body. In the daytime, troops of a dozen or more Woolly Monkeys commonly feed high in trees on fruits and leaves, often with Capuchins and Howlers. In captivity, often inactive, short-lived.

Night
Monkey

NIGHT MONKEYS are bushy-tailed, soft-furred (13 in.) monkeys of central and northern South America. They are called Owl Monkeys because of their large eyes and facial markings and because, unlike other monkeys, they are nocturnal. In daytime, they sleep in hollow trees.

Brown Capuchin

Black-capped Capuchin

White-throated Capuchin

Spider Monkey

SPIDER MONKEYS (18 in.) have a long tail and slim arms and legs. The end of the tail lacks hair. Using only the tail, they cling to limbs and pick up objects. Groups of Spider Monkeys move through treetops with great speed. Several females may be caged with one male.

CAPUCHINS (12–15 in.) are the organ grinder's monkey. Because they coil their long tail in a ring, they are often called Ring-tailed Monkeys. They live in troops. Capuchins are fascinating to watch—but usually are difficult to keep as pets and eventually become unmanageable.

NEW WORLD MONKEYS 31

Squirrel Monkey

SQUIRREL MONKEYS (two species of tropical Central and South America) are small (12 in.) but have a long tail (16. in.). They eat fruit and insects; in captivity, eggs and canned meat.

Red Uakari

White Uakari

UAKARIS (wa-car-e) are semi-bald, wrinkly faced, 21-in. Amazon monkeys with chin whiskers, large, sunken eyes, a short tail. One species is red; another, nearly white. Uncommon, shy, and difficult to keep in captivity.

TITI MONKEYS (30 in.) have a small head, long woolly fur, and a very long prehensile tail used in climbing. Delicate and often shy, they do poorly in captivity, usually living only a few months. In the wild, eat insects, eggs, birds, fruits, and leaves.

Red Titi

SAKIS are gentle but delicate and difficult to keep. They require warm quarters and branches for exercise to keep them healthy. White-faced Sakis (22 in.) inhabit tropical forests of northern South America. Other kinds are the Monk, White-headed, and Red-backed.

White-faced Saki

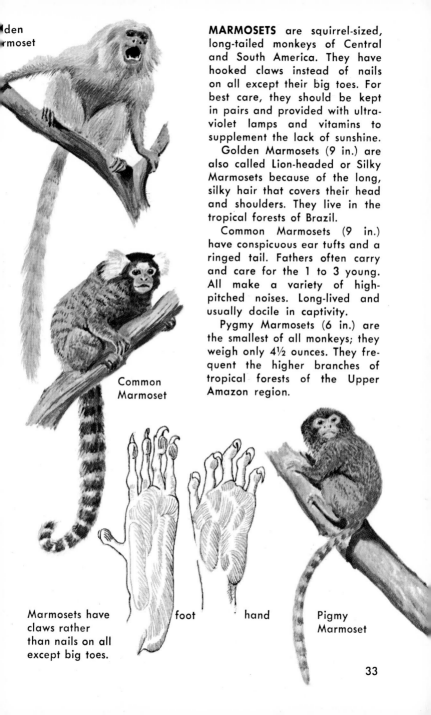

den
rmoset

MARMOSETS are squirrel-sized, long-tailed monkeys of Central and South America. They have hooked claws instead of nails on all except their big toes. For best care, they should be kept in pairs and provided with ultra-violet lamps and vitamins to supplement the lack of sunshine.

Golden Marmosets (9 in.) are also called Lion-headed or Silky Marmosets because of the long, silky hair that covers their head and shoulders. They live in the tropical forests of Brazil.

Common Marmosets (9 in.) have conspicuous ear tufts and a ringed tail. Fathers often carry and care for the 1 to 3 young. All make a variety of high-pitched noises. Long-lived and usually docile in captivity.

Pygmy Marmosets (6 in.) are the smallest of all monkeys; they weigh only 4½ ounces. They frequent the higher branches of tropical forests of the Upper Amazon region.

Common
Marmoset

Marmosets have
claws rather
than nails on all
except big toes.

foot   hand

Pigmy
Marmoset

33

Tarsier

Potto

Tree
Shrew

Galago

TREE SHREWS, from India, Malaya, and the Philippines, were originally classified as shrews. These chipmunk-sized primates with long tails, are carnivorous in the wild but eat fruit and other foods in zoos. Several will live together in a cage.

TARSIERS, rat-sized, weigh 3 to 5 ounces. In the bamboo thickets of the Philippines and East Indies, they feed at night on insects and lizards. Captives drink milk; eat lizards, mice, insects. Rare and short-lived in zoos.

COMMON POTTOS of West Africa are about the size of house cats. They live in trees where they eat leaves, fruit, insects, and lizards. Pottos sleep during the day and move as sluggishly as sloths.

GALAGOS, or Bush Babies (10 in.), are furry, thin-eared forest dwellers of Africa. All 4 species have long, bushy tails and are nocturnal. They tame readily; eat insects, cooked meats. They can curl and uncurl their ears.

Ring-tailed
Lemur

ngoose
ur

RING-TAILED LEMURS (body 30 in.; tail 18 in.) are one of about 16 species of primitive primates that live only on Madagascar. All are squirrel-like in habits, appearance, and size. Ring-tailed Lemurs are active during the day, do well in captivity, and are a popular zoo species. Young hang onto the adults as they run about the cage.

MONGOOSE LEMURS and Brown Lemurs (body 24 in.; tail 12 in.) are displayed in a few zoos. They move rapidly over their climbing perches and around the sides of their cage, staying off the floor. Lemurs eat vegetables and fruit, rarely meat.

RUFFED LEMURS (body 26 in.; tail 14 in.) are black and white with a collar or ruff about the neck. One form is red and black. This species normally feeds and moves about at night or in dusky light. Rarely displayed.

SLOW LORISES, of Indonesia and the Philippines, are slow, sluggish, 14-in. tree dwellers, active at dusk or dark. They curl up during the day to sleep. Fruit is their main zoo food. Lorises raise young in captivity.

Ruffed
Lemur

Slow
Loris

35

CARNIVORES are flesh-eating mammals with specialized teeth for grasping prey and shearing flesh. Some have lost the flesh-eating habit. Most are strong runners; many are good climbers. Bears, raccoons, weasels, civets, hyenas, cats, and dogs are carnivores.

BEARS are flat-footed, almost tail-less. Some feed extensively on fruits and insects. All except the Spectacled Bear of South America live in the Northern Hemisphere.

POLAR BEARS of northern snow and ice fields feed mostly on seals and fish; males attain a weight of 1,000 lbs. Excellent swimmers, they enjoy frolicking in a pool, summer or winter, and seemingly suffer no more from heat than do cats or other caged animals. The Polar Bear's zoo diet consists of horse meat, fish, and bread, to which vitamin supplements are added.

Polar Bear

BROWN BEARS have a pronounced hump between their shoulders, long claws on the front feet, and a hollow face. Several kinds live in the northern part of North America and Eurasia. These include the largest carnivorous land mammals— 8 ft. in length, 4 ft. high at the shoulder, and 9 ft. high standing on their hind feet. At birth they are rat-sized and helpless.

Grizzly Bears, slightly smaller but otherwise similar to Brown Bears, live farther south in North America. Both kinds are usually kept outdoors in moated cages the year around. Bears may sleep for long periods in winter but do not hibernate. Adult bears may eat 20 lbs. of meat, bread, and vegetables a day. Visitors should never offer them food.

Grizzly
Bear

Brown
Bear

Black Bear
(two color phases)

BLACK BEARS (about 5 ft. long) are a North American species, usually black in color but sometimes brown, cinnamon, or nearly white. Their claws are not especially long. Black Bears feed principally on fruits, insects, small animals, and honey, but are omnivorous. During the cold winter months, they are often dormant, arousing only to eat. During the dormancy, females give birth to cubs, each less than a pound—less than ½ per cent of mother's weight.

SUN BEARS (4 ft. long) are the smallest bears and usually weigh less than 100 lbs. They live in dense jungles of Southeast Asia. Excellent climbers. Crescent on chest may resemble rising sun, hence name.

SLOTH BEARS (5½ ft. long) are slow-moving, shaggy-coated bears of Ceylon and India. Their diet in nature includes honey, termites, sugar cane, rodents. Excellent climbers, feed in trees as well as on ground.

Sun
Bear

Sloth
Bear

Giant Panda

cub

GIANT PANDAS live in the dense bamboo jungles, 5,000 to 14,000 ft. above sea level, in Tibet and China. Adults are nearly 6 ft. long, weigh 200 to 380 lbs. Captives are fed bamboo shoots, their principal food in the wild, supplemented with corn stalks, twigs, and even a porridge of oats, milk, and cod-liver oil. Giant Pandas are shown in zoos in China and elsewhere presently only in Moscow and in London. Giant Pandas are now considered close relatives of and in the same family as the bears.

RACCOON AND WEASEL FAMILIES include a number of small mammals kept in zoos. Raccoons, Lesser Pandas, Kinkajous, and Coatimundis have a long tail (usually ringed) and are flat-footed. Weasels, skunks, badgers, otters, and mink have scent glands and luxuriant pelts.

LESSER PANDAS, members of the raccoon family, live in forests above 6,000 ft. in the Himalaya Mountains. They are the size of house cats but have a heavier tail and are excellent climbers. In captivity, Lesser Pandas are fed bamboo leaves and a variety of fruits and vegetables.

Lesser Panda

WEASELS, RACCOONS AND ALLIES

Kinkajou

Coatimundi

Raccoon

Hog-
nosed
Skunk

Striped   Spotted

KINKAJOUS (20 in.), monkey-like relatives of the Raccoon, live in Central and South America. In captivity, they do well but can not withstand cold. The long tail is used as an extra hand when climbing in trees where they move about with great dexterity. They feed on fruits and honey. Often called Honey Bears.

COATIMUNDIS (24 in.), also called Coatis and Chulas, have long, black-ringed tails. They move about noisily, searching for worms or grubs with their long snout. Coatis travel and feed during the day, often in groups of 30 or more. They live from South America north to Arizona. Often partially tamed.

RACCOONS (32 in.) are flat-footed, black-masked, ring-tailed mammals of the Americas. They feed on crayfish, frogs, insects, fruits, and rodents. Washing their food in water is not a necessity, but they may do so. Dog food, horse meat, fruit, and vitamins provide a satisfactory cage diet. Raccoons often use hollow trees as dens.

HOG-NOSED SKUNK (16 in.) is the largest skunk in North America. Uses hoglike snout to root in ground for insects. Like all skunks, scent is stored in two glands under tail. Striped Skunks (13 in.) are common in meadows and fence rows. Spotted Skunks (10 in.) are really striped but short bands give illusion of spots.

WOLVERINES are large (32 in.; 35 lbs.) weasels of North American and Eurasian boreal forests. They kill game of all sizes—squirrels to deer. In captivity one will consume nearly 4 lbs. of meat a day. Large cages permitting exercise are most suitable. Fur is used to line parka hoods, for it sheds moisture.

TAYRAS are tree-climbing, weasel-like animals of the American tropics. Although over 3 ft. long, a third of this is tail. They are short-legged and black except for the lighter colored head and neck. Tayras are active in the daytime. They hunt in trees for the small mammals, birds, and fruit on which they feed.

HONEY BADGERS (28 in.), or Ratels, are fond of honey and raid nests of ground-dwelling bees, often following birds called Honeyguides to find these nests. Honey Badgers live in Africa and southern Asia. Among the several other kinds of badgers, all short-legged, flat-bodied, and excellent diggers, are European, American, and Sand badgers.

RIVER OTTERS are finely furred, aquatic, weasel-like mammals. Their body is streamlined and their feet webbed. Some otters are clawless. Exhibited species include: American River Otter (about 2½ ft. long) and the Amazon Flat-tailed and African Giant otters (both about 5 ft. long). Captives eat fish or horse meat mixed with vegetables. In the wild, the African Giant Otter eats mainly shellfish.

Wolverine

Tayra

Honey Badger

Amazon
Flat-tailed Otter

American River Otter

Binturong

Masked Palm Civet

Mongoose

Meerkat

BINTURONGS, largest of the civets, are 4½ ft. long, but nearly half of this length is a bushy, grasping tail used in climbing. They live in the tropical forests of southeastern Asia, and they feed mainly on fruit.

CIVETS AND MONGOOSES are slender-muzzled, long-tailed animals of southern Europe, Africa, Asia. Their scent-gland secretion is used in perfumes.

PALM CIVETS are cat-sized climbers of the forests of Asia and equatorial Africa. Civets, like skunks, can discharge a nauseating fluid from scent glands. All palm civets, including the Masked, do well in zoos.

MONGOOSES (24 in.) are coarse-haired animals of Eurasia and Africa. Good rat killers, they have been introduced for this purpose and then become pests. Laws prevent import to U.S. Related Meerkat also banned.

Spotted Hyena

Striped Hyena

HYENAS are nocturnal, 4–5 ft., doglike animals with large heads, weak hindquarters, and a generally ungraceful appearance. The short tail is frequently carried between the legs. Hyenas are sometimes called Laughing Hyenas because they make a variety of noises resembling cries, cackles, barks, and laughs. These scavengers pick over the scraps that remain after the feasts of other animals, especially of lions. They even eat leftover bones, using their strong teeth and powerful jaws to crush the bones of antelopes and buffaloes.

SPOTTED HYENAS, of Central and South Africa, have short, rounded ears and dark spots over most of the body. Young are darker and more spotted. Shy and retiring, they do not display well.

STRIPED HYENAS, found from India to North Africa, have a striped body and long ears. Brown Hyenas of South Africa, not often shown in zoos, have stripes only on legs and coarse hair on body.

HYENAS   43

CATS of many different sizes and markings occur world-wide except in Australia. All have sharp, shearing teeth and claws that retract into sheaths (except Cheetahs). Cats fit into three groups: lions and other large cats that roar but cannot purr; smaller cats (lynxes, ocelots, and others) that purr; Cheetahs that give barking howls and birdlike chirps. In captivity, cats are fed raw meat fortified with vitamins and minerals.

Lion

male

FUR PATTERNS OF CATS

Lion   Tiger   Siberian Tiger   Leopard

LIONS are among the most impressive carnivorous mammals and attract much attention in zoos. They reach maturity at 5 or 6 years. Males have a mane that appears at about 1½ years. Manes in zoo animals may be bushier than those in the wild since they are not torn by the brush. Nubian Lions lack manes.

Lions breed readily in captivity, producing cubs with spots that usually disappear in about 6 months. Lions begin to be old at age 10. In captivity, however, they have lived for more than 25 years.

Lions hunt and travel in groups called prides. They live in much of Africa and formerly also from Greece to India. Now only a few remain in India. Lions prefer the open, grassy plains and avoid the dense, tropical forests. They prey mainly on hoofed mammals—zebras, wildebeests, antelopes, even buffaloes. In hunting, they charge but do not pursue long if they fail to make the kill.

Adult males weigh to 425 lbs., one reportedly over 500. Females are smaller, weighing to about 250 lbs.

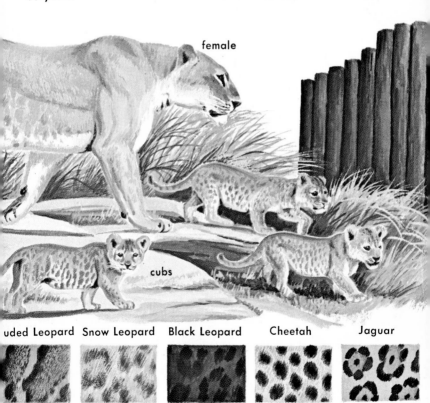

female

cubs

uded Leopard　Snow Leopard　Black Leopard　Cheetah　Jaguar

Bengal Tiger

male

TIGERS are the large cats with prominent, black or brown, stripes. They are common in jungles of India and Java, but range as far as the snowy, forested mountains of Siberia. Siberian Tigers usually have pale, long, thick fur. Bengal Tigers of the tropics have shorter fur and brighter colors. Mature males usually weigh around 400 lbs.; a Siberian Tiger was reported to reach 650 lbs. Large animals are about 3 ft. high at the shoulders.

Tigers usually are solitary hunters. Very powerful, they attack animals as large as young elephants, water buffaloes, and crocodiles. Tigers are good swimmers and enjoy water, often entering to cool off. In captivity, they do not live as long as lions nor produce and rear young as successfully. Cubs weigh between 2 to 3 lbs. at birth. They mature in about 4 years. A male tiger and female lion may produce a tigon; the reverse, a ligon. Such hybrids occur only in zoos.

female and cubs

Leopard
(two color phases)

Snow
Leopard

Clouded Leopard

LEOPARDS, infrequently called Panthers, are forest inhabitants of Asia and Africa. They are not especially large cats, weighing between 100 and 200 lbs., but are good hunters, using stealth and ambush. Usually they hunt at night. The color is variable, but most commonly Leopards are yellowish with four or five dark-brown spots in rosettes. Black individuals are common in India. Different colors and patterns may occur in Leopard cubs of the same litter.

SNOW LEOPARDS (3 ft.) inhabit the cold parts of the Himalaya and Altai mountains. Their coat is dense and long. Zoo quarters may need cooling in summer to keep them comfortable. Also called the Ounce.

CLOUDED LEOPARDS, of Southeast Asia, have a mixture of spots and stripes. Mature animals weigh less than 50 lbs. and are about 3 ft. long. Shy and retiring in captivity; active at night in the wild.

Jaguar

JAGUARS, largest (5 ft.) of the American cats, weigh up to 300 lbs. They can roar, like Lions and Tigers. Jaguars prey on a variety of animals, including fish and the Capybara (p. 62). They live along waterways in jungles of tropical America. Excellent climbers and leapers, they are kept in well-barred cages, rarely in moated cages. Kittens heavily spotted at birth. Black phases common; occasionally nearly white ones occur.

CHEETAHS (5 ft.), most unusual of the cats, are doglike in appearance, make barking howls and, unlike all other cats, have no sheaths into which claws can retract. They live in open country from southern Asia to Africa. Cheetahs can run as fast as 70 miles per hour for short distances, enabling them to catch the swiftest of the antelopes. In India they are trained as hunters. Seldom reproduce in captivity; young are difficult to raise.

Cheetah

Caracal

Serval

Ocelot

Golden Cat

CARACALS (3 ft.), found in deserts from Africa to India, have pointed, tufted ears. Good hunters of small game, they weigh up to 40 lbs. In zoos, require heated quarters during cold months. Caracals were used by Arabians as hunting cats.

SERVALS (2½ ft.) are long-legged, short-tailed African cats. They are yellowish with bold black stripes and spots. Servals prowl at night in marshes or along banks. They rarely reproduce in captivity.

OCELOTS (3 ft.), commonest cats of tropical America, are short-legged tree-dwellers. They are sometimes called Tiger Cats because of dark spots, blotches, and rings. Ocelots tame easily.

GOLDEN CATS (3 ft.), found from Tibet to Sumatra, are usually reddish brown, but some are spotted, others black. Another species lives in west-central Africa. Often displayed in zoos.

SMALL CATS 49

Lynx

Bobcat

Mountain Lion

Jaguarundi

LYNXES (2½ ft.) are broad-footed, stump-tailed cats with prominent ear tufts and a black-tipped tail. Young spotted. Lynxes hunt at night, preying mainly on rabbits. Found in northern parts of the New and Old Worlds, they can be kept outdoors.

MOUNTAIN LIONS, also called Panthers, Cougars, Pumas, and other names, are a solid tan or brown. The cubs are striped or spotted. Found only in North and South America, these large cats (to 8 ft.; 200 lbs.) scream; Old World lions roar.

BOBCATS, also called Wildcats or Bay Lynxes, are bobtailed, like the Lynx, but are slightly smaller, have smaller feet, and shorter ear tufts. Bobcats live in many parts of North America. They feed mainly on rodents and birds; sometimes eat vegetables.

JAGUARUNDIS (3½-4 ft.) have short legs, a long tail, and a slim body. They live in the tropics from southernmost United States to South America. Jaguarundis vary in color from rusty red (often called Eyra) to grayish black and solid black.

THE DOG FAMILY is world-wide in distribution. Members have long muzzles, a bushy tail, and prominent claws; all are good runners. Most do well in captivity. Some are nocturnal, hence sluggish in the daytime. They are fed dog food or horse meat, with supplements.

WOLVES (Timber or Gray), largest members of the family, are 4½ ft. long, weigh up to 175 lbs. They live in cold regions of North America and Eurasia. Wolves mate for life, and pups remain with parents a year or more. Tend to be quarrelsome.

COYOTES (3 ft.) live in sparsely wooded regions of North America; are most abundant in the West. Sometimes called Prairie Wolves, they usually weigh less than 60 lbs. They make a variety of eerie howls. Coyotes will eat nearly anything. Pups number up to 12 per litter.

DHOLES (Asiatic Wild Dogs or Red Dogs) are sociable, frequently hunting in packs of as many as 20. Pups are dusky gray. Dholes (3 ft.) live from Russia to Korea and southward to Java. May breed with domestic dogs; U.S. importation prohibited.

JACKALS (2½ ft.) are found in Asia and Africa. In habits and characteristics, they are the counterparts of the North American Coyote. They often feast on what is left after the big cats have made a kill. There are several kinds: Yellow or Asiatic, Black-backed, and Side-striped.

Wolf

Coyote

Yellow Jackal

Dhole

51

Red Fox

Gray Fox

RED FOXES (2 ft.) persist in northern Asia, Europe, and North America. In addition to reddish-colored coats, there are blacks, silvers (black hair tipped with white), and "crosses" (reddish with black). Several foxes can be penned together.

FENNECS (1–1½ ft.) are large-eared, desert foxes of North Africa and the Near East. Kit Foxes of North America's western deserts are similar. Both are shy. Fennecs do best in zoos.

ARCTIC FOXES (2–2½ ft.) have white coats, matching the snow of the Arctic tundra, but some are always bluish-gray (Blue Foxes). Their small ears are nearly hidden in fur. Usually do not live long in captivity.

GRAY FOXES (2 ft.), found in North American wooded regions, can climb trees. They feed on small mammals, birds, and berries, and frequently dig burrows. Their grayish-red coat and black-tipped tail is characteristic. Like most foxes, active at night.

Fennec

Arctic Fox

Kit Fox

Big-eared Fox

Dingo

BIG-EARED FOXES (1½ ft.) are also called Bat-eared and Long-eared foxes. In their native southern and eastern Africa, these animals feed on small mammals, reptiles, birds, and insects. They dig dens for shelter and rearing of the young.

MANED WOLVES (4 ft.), from the South American pampas, are strangely proportioned. They have stiltlike legs, a short tail, and long ears on a foxlike head. They eat lizards, snakes, rodents, and fruits. Though not common in zoos, they apparently require no special care.

DINGOES, or Australian Wild Dogs, look like large, reddish-colored, domesticated dogs. They cannot lay their ears down, however, and they yelp or howl rather than bark. Dingoes are the only non-marsupial meat-eating mammals in Australia.

CAPE OR AFRICAN HUNTING DOGS are large (3–3½ ft.), powerful hunters with rounded ears, a spotted body, and long legs. In their native Africa, they commonly run in packs of 30 or more, killing antelope and other big game. They remain unfriendly in captivity.

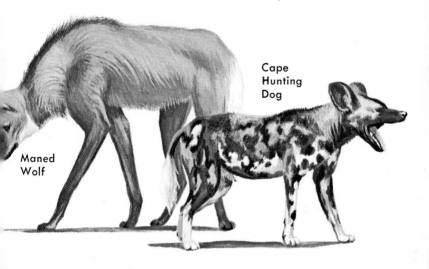

Cape Hunting Dog

Maned Wolf

FIN-FOOTED (PINNIPED) carnivores are modified to live in the water. Their flippers aid them in swimming; their short, thick fur provides insulation; their torpedo-shaped body helps them glide through the water. Includes seals, sea lions, elephant seals, and walruses.

ELEPHANT SEALS are large, fat, and docile in captivity. Their long nose droops many inches below their mouth, somewhat like an elephant's trunk. This snout is partially inflated as the animal exhales. Males may be 18 ft. long and weigh 2½ tons. They live in Pacific coastal waters, north to southern California.

SEA LIONS can turn their paddle-like hind flippers forward and use them as "feet" to pull themselves out of the water to sun or to "walk" on land. The California Sea Lion is common in zoos. Males may weigh 600 lbs.; females, 200. They bark loudly. Males eat about 8 lbs. of fish a day; females, 4.

California
Sea Lion

Elephant
Seal

WALRUSES live in waters of the Arctic Circle. Males have larger tusks than females and weigh more—up to 1½ tons. Their upper lips are covered with stiff bristles. Adults are wrinkled and nearly hairless; young have a thin coat of coarse hair. Although their size and unusual appearance attracts attention, they require much care and are not often kept in zoos. A 1,000-pound animal may eat 40 lbs. of fish (preferably filleted) and clams per day. Before being fed to a Walrus, the food is enriched with vitamins and minerals.

HARBOR SEALS are small (length, about 5 ft.; weight, about 200 lbs.) and light colored. They are shy, have difficulty moving on land, and usually remain in the water, mostly submerged. For these reasons, Harbor Seals are not commonly kept in zoos, though they are interesting and always attract attention when displayed. In the coastal waters where they live, seals feed on fishes, mollusks, and crustaceans. In captivity, two daily feedings totaling 5 lbs. of fish, some stuffed with vitamin capsules, will suffice.

California
Sea Lion

Walrus

Harbor
Seal

55

RODENTS, mostly small mammals and excellent gnawers, are found on every continent and from the tropics to the Arctic. Not only are there many kinds but many individuals, because most rodents mature rapidly and breed frequently. Nearly all rodents are active at night and hide or sleep during the daytime. These rodents are difficult to display in zoos. Some can be kept active in the daytime in cages that are dark except for small red lights. Many are kept in cages with glass fronts in small mammal houses where climatic conditions can be controlled throughout the year (pp. 60-61).

BEAVERS are large (2½–4 ft.), water-dwelling rodents with valuable fur coats. They feed on bark, cattails, and aquatic vegetation. Beaver pools with their beaver houses intrigue zoo visitors as much as do the animals. Beavers sleep or are sluggish during the day, however, and unless the pens are darkened or the animals have adjusted to daytime conditions, their activities are not seen by the visitors. North American and European beavers are much alike. Leaves and branches are a suitable food, but a variety of vegetables can be substituted.

North American Beaver

webbed foot

flat tail

PORCUPINES (2½ ft.) have hair modified into sharp, strong spines, called quills. These spines, like all hair, are shed periodically. They cannot be thrown but do pull out easily and often lodge in the flesh of attackers. Barbs make the spines difficult to remove from the flesh. Porcupines gnaw on bark, roots, and fruits. North American porcupines often climb high into trees and may stay there for days while feeding on the inner bark. At birth the single young is large and already covered with spines. Few animals prey on porcupines, but the weasel-like Fisher flips the porcupine over and attacks its unprotected belly.

Crested Porcupines have nearly 2 ft. long spines on the back that form a crest when the animal is disturbed. These spines, frequently erected and rattled or vibrated to warn potential attackers, are smooth or grooved and lack the burs or barbs on spines of North American Porcupines. Eurasian and African porcupines usually den in burrows dug by other animals. Porcupines of Malayan region have shorter spines and only at rear.

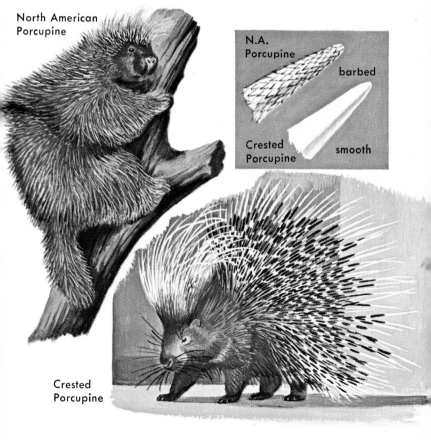

North American Porcupine

N.A. Porcupine

barbed

Crested Porcupine

smooth

Crested Porcupine

Antelope Ground Squirrel

Thirteen-lined Ground Squirrel

Black-tailed Prairie Dog

GROUND SQUIRRELS rest and nest in underground burrows but are active on warm days on the surface. Thirteen-lined Ground Squirrels (6 in.) live on open prairies, pastures, and even golf courses of midwestern North America. They sit erect alongside their holes, alert for enemies. Antelope Ground Squirrels (5 in), with white side stripes and white tail, are desert inhabitants. Eurasian Ground Squirrels, or Susliks (10 in.), are found on sandy wastelands and give a high-pitched warning whistle.

PRAIRIE DOGS are squirrel-like rodents that live in colonies (dog towns) on prairies and in mountain meadows of western North America. They live below ground in deep burrows. Above ground, they sun and feed on grasses and seeds. A mound of soil as much as a foot high built around each entrance, serves as a lookout platform and keeps out rainwater. In winter, prairie dogs hibernate in underground chambers. Of the several species, the Black-tailed (12 in.) is the one most commonly shown in zoos.

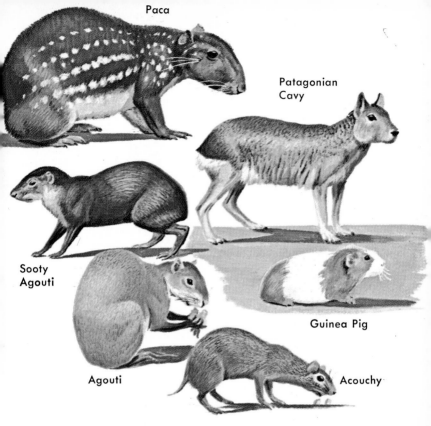

Paca

Patagonian Cavy

Sooty Agouti

Guinea Pig

Agouti

Acouchy

PACAS AND AGOUTIS, from South America north to southern Mexico, have long hind feet with hooflike toes and a scarcely visible tail. They live in colonies.

Pacas (26 in.), conspicuously spotted, dig burrows for shelters and nests, often in banks of rivers or lakes. Agoutis (20 in.), the size of small rabbits and with no visible tail, travel by hopping or running. They tame readily. Acouchies (14 in.) are similar but have a visible tail. All eat green vegetation and roots; in zoos, fruit, seeds, and bread.

PATAGONIAN CAVIES (28 in.), native to southern South America, are much like large jackrabbits, dashing about in hopping runs. Often they are called "hares." Cavies do well in captivity, thriving on a variety of foods including plant materials, and become quite tame. Prominent lashes protect their eyes from the sun's glare. Their fur is long and dense. Patagonian Cavies rest and nest in burrows dug themselves or by other animals. The short-legged Guinea-pig (10 in.) is also a Cavy.

Woodchuck   African Giant Rat

WOODCHUCKS (20 in.), the Groundhogs of eastern U.S. and Canada, dig underground homes near rock piles and woods or in fields and pastures where they forage. In western U.S., the related Yellow-bellied Marmot lives in mountain valleys; others live in Eurasia, Alaska, and Canada.

CHIPMUNKS (6 in.), brightly colored, striped squirrels, inhabit forests or forest edges in parts of North America, Siberia, and northern Japan. Active only during the day, they feed mostly on nuts and seeds. Some are tree-climbers; others prefer to scamper about on the ground.

AFRICAN GIANT RATS are nearly 3 ft. long and more than half the length is a nearly hairless tail. The tail is used as a balancing organ when the animals run or climb. African Giant Rats are omnivorous and carry food in their large cheek pouches, hence their name, Pouched Rat.

SPINY MICE (3 in.) have spines and modified hair on the back and sides. These docile mice, native to Africa and India, are now commonly kept as pets. The tail is easily broken and can never be replaced. Spiny Mice eat a variety of foods: seeds, fruits, and mouse chow.

Spiny Mouse

Eastern Chipmunk

60 RODENTS

Banner-tailed Kangaroo Rat

Jerboa

Clawed Gerbil

KANGAROO RATS (5 in.) have short front feet and can jump about on their long hind feet, like miniature kangaroos. They have cheek pouches in which they carry seeds to store in their nests. Kangaroo Rats are incompatible, hence only one can be kept in each cage.

JERBOAS (5 in.), of North African and Asian deserts, have long ears and a tufted tail. They are good jumpers but dig burrows in the sand and stay in them during the daytime. Clawed Gerbils, or Jirds (5 in.), are also exhibited in zoos and sometimes used as laboratory animals.

CHINCHILLAS are squirrel-sized rodents with silky fur used in making expensive coats, capes, and stoles. They are now rare in their native western South America but are raised on fur farms. Chinchillas reproduce in captivity, frequently having two litters of one to four young each year.

GIANT TREE SQUIRREL, the Ratufa or Malabar, of southeastern Asia, is about 3 ft. long. Because of its large size and daytime activities, it is perhaps the most frequently displayed of tree squirrels. In its native jungles, the Giant Tree Squirrel is noisy and conspicuous.

Giant Tree Squirrel

Chinchilla

NUTRIA, or Coypu, is a South American rodent that lives in and near streams, lakes, and swamps. It is an excellent swimmer. The Nutria has coarse guard hairs and fine, soft underfur, used in making capes, coats, and other fur apparel. It is raised on fur farms in North America. A Nutria's thick, round, almost hairless tail is nearly as long as its 1½ to 2 ft. body. Captive nutrias have been liberated or escaped and have established colonies in the wild in many parts of the world. Because they eat many kinds of green vegetation, they are sometimes pests. They are active during the day, thus are good zoo animals.

CAPYBARA, the largest of all rodents, is pig-sized and may weigh 160 lbs. In its native South America, the Capybara is usually found along streams and lakes in family groups of a dozen or more. Sometimes called Water Hog, it is an excellent swimmer and may take to the water to escape enemies. Natives often kill them for food. In the wild, the Capybara feeds mainly on water plants and grasses. In zoos, they are fed vegetables, hay, and bread. This big, slow-moving, good-natured rodent utters low clicking noises or sharp whistles. It is more active at dusk and during the night. Capybaras are not common in zoos.

Capybara

Nutria

62

SLOTHS (2 ft.) are members of a group sometimes called toothless mammals. Some have no teeth and others, including sloths, have peglike, nearly functionless, teeth. Their coarse, strawlike fur may be green with growths of algae. Sloths live in the rainy jungles of the American tropics. They feed on leaves, creep along branches, and even sleep hanging upside down. They are awkward on the ground. Two-toed Sloths have 2 claws on each front foot; Three-toed Sloths, 3.

Two-toed Sloth

GIANT ANTEATERS (4 ft.) are long-haired, bushy-tailed, jungle dwellers of Central and South America. During their daytime naps they curl into a ball. They use the long claws on their powerful front legs to tear open termite nests. Then a nearly foot-long tongue flicks up the insects. In zoos they are fed a puree of milk, boiled eggs, and meat.

AARDVARKS (4½–5 ft.), piglike African mammals, have large ears that are folded down when the animals dig into the nests of termites and ants. A long sticky tongue gathers up the insects. Excavated nests also serve as homes. In captivity Aardvarks, which have no grinding teeth, eat finely chopped foods and cooked cereals.

Giant Anteater

Aardvark

63

EVEN-TOED hoofed mammals (Artiodactyla) support their weight on two toes (their 3rd and 4th toes). Many are cud-chewers (ruminants); some have horns or antlers. Included are hippos, pigs, camels, deer, cattle, antelopes and giraffes.

HIPPOPOTAMUSES live in the rivers and river valleys of tropical Africa. Wild hippos spend much of the day-time in water with only their eyes and nostrils protruding. They are excellent swimmers and floaters and can even walk along the river bottom. On land they can gallop when necessary.

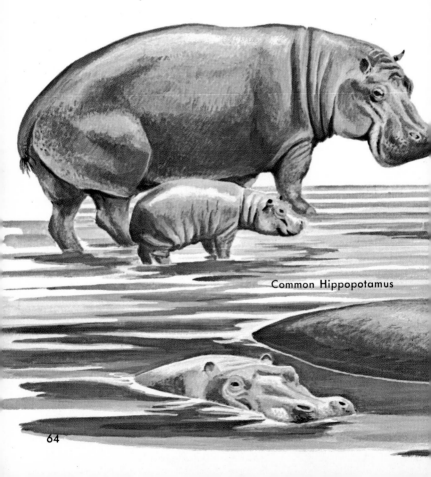

Common Hippopotamus

Pygmy
Hippopotamus

COMMON HIPPOPOTAMUS (12–15 ft.) is the second largest land animal, ranking after elephants. Bulls usually weigh between 3,500 and 5,000 lbs. In captivity, they are docile and readily breed. Some captives live over 40 years. In zoos, hippopotamuses thrive on daily rations of hay (80 to 100 lbs.), diced vegetables (several quarts), and grain (about 10 lbs. in pellet form).

PYGMY HIPPOPOTAMUS (5–6 ft.) lives along streams of the forested area of western Africa, but it is not as fond of water as the Common Hippo. Wild Pygmy Hippos are quite secretive, usually foraging at night. At one time they were uncommon in zoos. Captives eat about 1/5 as much as Common Hippos and sometimes become unruly. Many never weigh more than 400 lbs.

Bush Pig

Collared Peccary

Babirusa

Wart Hog

BUSH PIGS, or Red River Hogs (4½ ft.), have a distinctive bright reddish coat which contrasts with their white mane, white eye rings, and long ear tufts. They weigh about 200 lbs. Bush Pigs live in small herds in African forests. No pigs can be imported into the U.S. because of swine diseases, hence are not shown in American zoos.

BABIRUSAS (3 ft.) have unusual tusks (canine teeth). In the male the upper tusks grow out through the lip and then curve over the forehead, reaching a length of as much as 17 in. Lower tusks grow alongside. The long tusks resemble antlers, so these jungle dwellers of Burma and the Celebes are sometimes called Pig-deer. Uncommon in zoos.

COLLARED PECCARIES (3 ft.) are wild, piglike animals of Central America north to Arizona. Adults rarely weigh more than 65 lbs. In captivity, they are fed alfalfa, vegetables, fruit, and some meat—a diet suitable for all swine. White-lipped Peccaries, which have a white streak from the chin to the eye, live in the American tropics.

WART HOGS (3½ ft.) have grotesque warty bumps on their scooped-out face, large tusks, small eyes, and a nearly hairless body. Found in Africa, they sleep in holes dug by other animals and feed principally on grasses and vegetable matter. They display well in zoos, and many become gentle. Usually produce piglets in captivity.

CAMELS (10 ft.) have been domesticated as beasts of burden longer than any other mammals and carry 400 to 600 lbs. as far as 30 miles a day. The humps store fat that may be utilized for water. Camels are hardy in captivity; water, fences, or a moat are effective barriers.

BACTRIAN CAMELS are two-humped. They are domesticated in Asia where some are still wild in the Gobi Desert. In zoos, they eat hays and grains with mineral and vitamin supplements.

ARABIAN CAMELS are one-humped. Today, found only in domestication, they may live as long as 28 years but usually less. The Dromedary is a long-legged, riding-type of Arabian camel.

Bactrian Camel

Arabian Camel

Llama

SOUTH AMERICAN "CAMELS" are the Llamas, Alpacas, Guanacos, and Vicuñas. All feed on grasses and chew a cud but have only a three-chambered stomach, like camels, not four-chambered like other cud-chewers. They have an unusual habit of spitting when annoyed, which makes it difficult to display them in some zoos. Llamas and Alpacas are domesticated. Captives eat 4 lbs. or less of alfalfa and grains per day.

LLAMAS (4–5 ft.), domesticated forms of Guanacos, are commonly used as beasts of burden, carrying packs 15 to 20 miles a day for 20 days in a row. They are rarely ridden since they balk at heavy loads. The fleece is used for cloth, meat for food, hides for sandals, droppings for fuel. In zoos, usually one male Llama is penned with several females and their young.

Alpaca

Guanaco

Vicuña

ALPACAS (3–4 ft.) have fleecy wool that may grow 2 ft. long and touch the ground. Although not as fine as that of Vicuña, the wool is in great demand. Alpacas are smaller than Llamas but are also a domesticated form of the Guanaco. They are bred for wool instead of transport. In the wild, Alpacas live mostly above 12,000 ft., higher than Llamas.

GUANACOS (5 ft.) inhabit many parts of the pampas and Andes southward from Bolivia and across the plains of Patagonia nearly to the southernmost tip of South America. Wary and seldom seen, they are becoming rarer because of hunting and because their preferred ranges are being fenced off. They once lived in herds of 200 or 300; now the herds are much smaller.

VICUÑAS (4½ ft.) live in small herds, high in the Andes. Over-hunting almost eliminated these animals, but they are now protected. Vicuña males weigh less than 150 lbs. The soft, fine fleece is used in expensive coats. Males fight with females in captivity, so the sexes are penned separately. Fighting occurs in the wild when territory of a group's dominant male is challenged.

ALPACAS, VICUÑAS, GUANACOS 69

THE DEER FAMILY contains the only mammals with antlers of solid bone that grow out from the skull under a layer of living skin (the velvet). Each year bucks shed old antlers and grow new ones. Female Reindeer and Caribou have antlers, too. Chevrotains are a distinct family, separate from the deer family.

WHITE-TAILED DEER occur over much of North America and vary from the dog-sized Florida Key Deer to 250 lb. bucks of northern states. Spotted fawns are born in late spring. The white underside of the tail becomes conspicuous when the tail is raised. White-tails browse on leaves, fruits, and acorns; in captivity, they eat hay and grains; need salt. Antlered males may injure others in the pen.

MULE DEER is a western American species slightly larger than White-tailed and having a different arrangement of branches (tines) on the antlers. Antlers increase in size with increased vigor of the buck. After a male passes his prime, the antlers become shorter but remain heavy. Part or all of the top of the tail is black. One kind of Mule Deer near the Pacific Coast is called the Blacktailed Deer.

White-tailed Deer

Mule Deer

fa

Red Brocket

Asian Chevrotain

CHEVROTAINS OR MOUSE DEER are small, not much larger than rabbits (weight, as little as 6 lbs.; height, 12 in.). Water Chevrotains of Central Africa live in marsh thickets; Asian Chevrotains, in thick forests. They lack antlers or horns.

BROCKETS, true deer of Central and South America, stand only 2 ft. high at the shoulders. The antlers are simple, unbranched spikes. Characteristic of the several species is the short tail and arched back. All live in the dense tropical forests.

MUNTJACS, or Barking Deer, weigh up to 40 lbs. and stand about 20 in. high. The bucks have spikelike antlers, forked at the tips, and a pair of protruding tusklike upper teeth. Muntjacs live in dense jungles, especially near streams, and are

difficult to discover. When alarmed, they make loud barking sounds. They browse on leaves, twigs, and bark. In zoos, they are fed hay and pellets. Several species occur in southern Asia. Muntjacs are difficult to obtain for many zoos.

buck

Muntjac

doe

Fallow Deer
(three color phases)

Sika
Deer

FALLOW DEER have a yellowish or reddish-brown coat spotted with white. Some individuals, however, are dark brown and lack spots; others are white. They are exceptional jumpers for their height (3 ft.). Although native to the Mediterranean countries, Fallow Deer have been introduced widely, from Sweden to New Zealand. All captive deer should have their hay diet supplemented with pellets of grain, yeast, salt, and molasses.

SIKA DEER are variable in color; some a solid color, others with light spots and are often called Spotted Deer. About 3 ft. high at the shoulders, they weigh between 150 and 200 lbs. White hairs at the base of the tail stand erect when the animals are alert. Sika Deer live along the eastern coast and offshore islands of Asia. They have been introduced into many countries and do well in captivity, though bucks may fight.

RED DEER are the Stag Deer hunted for centuries in Europe by nobility. Once common from western Russia and northern Africa across all of Europe, Red Deer have been mostly exterminated. Large stags (males) may weigh 300 lbs., rarely 500; hinds (females) are smaller. American Wapiti or "Elk" are so similar to Red Deer that some people consider them varieties of one species. Elk males (bulls) communicate with "bugle" sounds.

MOOSE, called Elk in Europe and Asia, live in northern forested regions of the New and the Old Worlds. Largest of the deer, they may weigh 1,800 lbs. and be 6 ft. high at the shoulders. The flattened palmate antlers spread 6 ft. or more and are shed each year. Moose live in marshy places and in nearby forests. They eat aquatic plants, leaves, and bark. Short-necked, they kneel to feed on low plants. Poor breeders in captivity.

Red Deer

Moose

PÈRE DAVID'S DEER have never been known as wild animals. These 4 ft., 500 lb. deer were "discovered" by Father David in the 1860's as captives in the gardens of the Summer Palace in Peking, China. During the Boxer Rebellion, this herd was destroyed except for about 50 individuals taken to England. These long-tailed, slender-antlered deer have done well enough in captivity so that there are now about 450 individuals in some 30 zoos and parks.

AXIS DEER are attractive, graceful deer native to India and Ceylon but now introduced into many other countries. Their conspicuous white spots account for the native name of Chital (spotted). Adults are about 3 ft. high at the shoulders, weigh 150 to 200 lbs. Their antlers have very few branches. They live in grassy jungles, never far from water and in herds of several hundreds. Axis Deer thrive in capitivity, particularly in warm areas. Antlered bucks may fight.

Père David's Deer

Axis Deer

buck

doe

SAMBAR DEER of several kinds are found from India to the Philippines. India Sambar, the largest, weighs nearly 700 lbs. It lives in grassy woodlands of hilly or mountainous areas. The massive antlers have only 3 branches. Sambars resemble American Wapiti, and also use mud wallows to protect themselves from biting insects. Bare spots below each eye are glands. Sambars do well in zoos but may become fat with inactivity. Fawns are not spotted.

ELD'S DEER, or Thamin, of southeastern Asia prefer open plains or swampy country, but they show well in zoos. Males stand about 4 ft. high at the shoulders and weigh over 200 lbs.; females are smaller. Fawns are spotted. Eld's Deer are sensitive to cold weather and resemble other deer from tropical countries in needing heated quarters in cold, winter regions. They are sometimes easily alarmed or startled. Antlers extend prominently over the brow.

Sambar Deer

Eld's Deer

Reindeer

Caribou

REINDEER are kinds of Caribou domesticated in northern Europe and Siberia and introduced into arctic North America. They pull sleds and provide milk, meat, and skin for clothing. In the wild they eat Reindeer Moss. They do poorly in most zoos.

CARIBOU, like Reindeer, live in the arctic regions and weigh up to 600 lbs. Both males and females have large antlers. Sometimes thousands of Caribou band together and make long migrations. Caribou generally do not fare well in captivity.

PRONGHORNS are an exclusively North American family and are not antelopes. They are plains and desert dwellers. Horns, present in both males and females, are shed annually. A bony core is beneath the horn.

Pronghorns are fast, nimble runners and can attain speeds of nearly 60 miles per hour. Males weigh over 100 lbs. and stand about 3 ft. at the shoulders. Pronghorns usually do not do well in captivity.

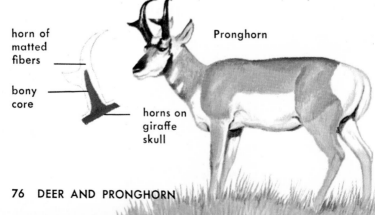

horn of matted fibers

bony core

horns on giraffe skull

Pronghorn

CATTLE, SHEEP, AND ANTELOPES, all of the family Bovidae, have horns that are never shed. They are formed over a bony core attached to the skull. These horns, usually present in both sexes, are added to each year. Size, shape, and configuration of horns varies.

BISON, or American Buffalo, have shaggy heads and humped backs. They may weigh more than a ton, the cows smaller than the bulls. In former times, thousands of these sociable animals gathered in herds. Some 60 million Bison roamed the plains and valleys from Mexico to western Canada and eastward to the Appalachians. Nearly all were killed, but under protection they are increasing. Wisent, or European Bison, are slightly larger than American Bison and exist today both in American and European zoos.

MUSK OXEN, rare in zoos, are shaggy-haired, cow-sized animals that live in the barren polar regions of North America. Their musky odor during the breeding season may be the basis for their name. Their long, heavy fur coats protect them from the snow and wind. For protection against wolves, they form a circle with their heads pointed out toward the attackers, with the calves inside the circle. Their horns, to 2 ft. long, and sharp hoofs are effective weapons. They eat willow leaves, mosses, and grass.

Bison

Musk Ox

YAKS are shaggy-coated, cattle-like animals of high mountain plateaus in Central Asia. Natives use them as beasts of burden, eat their meat, drink their pink milk, and weave with their fur. Long hair frequently covers their eyes and ears and forms a skirt around their legs, protecting them from the cold. In zoos, regardless of the temperature, Yaks do well. Domesticated Yaks grunt when overloaded, hence the name Grunting Oxen.

ANOAS, uncommon in captivity, are small buffalo of the Celebes. A white crescent on the throat and short horns are characteristic. These animals keep to the damp woods of remote mountains. They may be aggressive, even dangerous in the wild, and have attacked other animals in zoos. Anoas are sometimes called Dwarf Buffalo, since adult males are no larger than calves of domestic cattle. The larger Philippine Tamarou is nearly extinct.

Yak

Anoa, or
Dwarf
Buffalo

GAURS, sometimes called Seladangs, are large, powerful wild cattle that live in Indonesia. Bulls are frequently 6 ft. high at the shoulders. They have horns nearly 3 ft. long and a slightly developed dewlap, a fold of skin hanging from the throat. Gaurs live in small herds in grassy or hilly forest country. Gaurs have not been domesticated, and they do not do well in captivity. For this reason they are rarely seen in zoos.

WATER BUFFALOES, also called Arnas or Indian Buffaloes, are native to Indochina where they have been domesticated. They prefer grassy or marshy areas near rivers, in which they frequently submerge except for their heads. Ox-sized, they make fair draft animals and have been introduced into other countries. Cape or African Buffaloes of southern Africa have larger ears than Water Buffaloes and have never been domesticated.

Gaur

Water Buffalo

Cape Buffalo

CHAMOIS, also called Goat Antelopes (3-4 ft.), are sure-footed rock climbers of the Pyrenees, Alps, and other high mountains in southeastern Europe. Best known as a source for soft skins, or shammies. Chamois travel in herds, but old males are solitary. Do poorly in captivity, hence rare in zoos.

Chamois

Aoudads

AOUDADS, or Barbary Sheep (4–6 ft.), are the only sheeplike or goatlike animals of the African continent. They were once common in the rocky hills of the Atlas Mountains adjacent to the Barbary Coast. Although called sheep, Aoudads are more goatlike. Goats usually differ from wild sheep in having longer tails, a beard or goatee, and more twisted horns. Aoudads enjoy water but are able to withstand desert conditions. They do well in captivity, even living together in closely confined herds. In the wild, their herds consist of several family groups. In zoos, Aoudads thrive on alfalfa, fresh vegetables, and grains. Under favorable conditions lambs (usually one) are produced yearly by mature females.

MOUFLONS are the wild sheep of Europe. At one time almost exterminated, they are now present on several mountain ranges in Central Europe and on the Mediterranean islands of Sardinia and Corsica. Only about 27 in. at the shoulders, they are smaller than Bighorn Sheep, which in general they resemble.

HIMALAYAN TAHRS (3½ ft.) are goatlike animals with thick coats that protect against the cold of the Himalayas. They lack a goatee. Tahrs do well in zoos, producing kids regularly. Nilgiri Tahr of southern India and Arabian Tahr, less common in zoos, have shorter coats and smaller horns. Tahrs are wary and unapproachable in the wild but adjust quickly to captivity.

Himalayan Tahr

Mouflon

81

MARKHORS (4½ ft.), goats of southern Asia, live on rocky slopes where they are good climbers and jumpers. The horns are heavy and twisted in corkscrew spirals. Uncommon in zoos, but get along together in small herds when confined.

BIGHORNS (4½ ft.) are mountain-dwelling sheep of western North America. They travel in bands, but the rams (males) frequently keep apart. A few zoos have been successful in keeping and rearing Bighorns. Dall Sheep of Arctic America and Asia are similar but white.

IBEXES (4½ ft.) are the wild goats of Europe, North Africa, and parts of Asia. All of the several kinds prefer steep cliffs and rocky slopes of mountains. Ibexes still survive in remote parts of the Alps and Himalayas. Related to domestic goats.

Markhor

Asiatic Ibex

Bighorn

ANTELOPES are swift-running, browsing and grazing, horned animals of the grassland and bush of Africa and southern Asia. Horns, often present in both sexes, may be straight, sickle-shaped, or greatly twisted. Usually displayed indoors, at least in winter. They eat hay, grain-molasses-yeast pellets, and diced vegetables.

NYALAS (3 ft. at shoulder), members of the ringed or harnessed antelope group, have encircling, harness-like stripes on their body. They characteristically have erectile white hair on the back and a fringe of hairs on throat. Reddish coat browns with age. Nyalas live in isolated parts of southeastern Africa. Rare in zoos.

BONGOS live in West Africa and western Kenya where their stocky build aids them in pushing through the dense bamboo forests. Like the Eland but unlike other harnessed antelopes, both sexes of Bongos have horns. These beautiful 4 ft. animals are seldom seen in the wild, and only 1 pair is in a zoo at present.

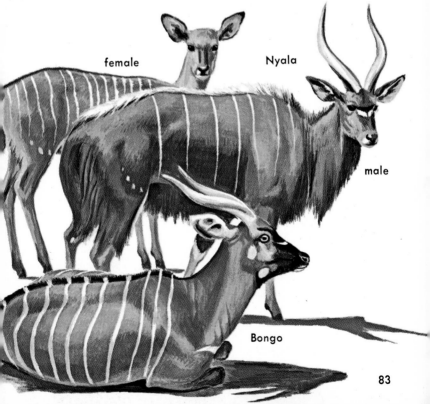

female

Nyala

male

Bongo

Common Eland

Sitatunga

Greater Kudu

ELANDS, the largest antelopes, live in the bush country and open woods of South Africa. Ox-like in build, they may be 6 ft. high at shoulders and weigh a ton. A herd may number 200. Both males and females have horns. Bulls have a large dewlap, humped shoulders. Elands have been tamed but have never been domesticated.

GREATER KUDUS, found now only in East Africa, are nearly Eland-size but have long (up to 5 ft.), spiraled horns. Unlike the shorter-horned Lesser Kudus, a prominent mane hangs from the throat. Good jumpers, they may clear an 8 ft. fence. To avoid detection, a Greater Kudu will stand silent and motionless.

SITATUNGAS (3½–4 ft. at shoulder), also called Marshbucks or Waterkoedoes, are West African swamp dwellers. Often rest almost completely submerged. Long hoofs enable them to walk through mud without sinking. Buck's horns may be 3 ft. long; females, hornless.

Nilgai

Lechwe's
Waterbuck

Sing-sing
Waterbuck

NILGAIS, or Blue Bulls, are closely related to African harnessed antelopes (p. 83), but they live on the open plains of India. They are the largest of Indian antelopes, standing about 4½ ft. at shoulders. Horns shorter than in other large antelopes, absent in females. There is a mane as well as a fringe on the throat.

WATERBUCKS have heavily ringed horns, present in males only. Sing-sing Waterbucks (3½– 4 ft.) live in marshy areas and also on hot, dry plains of equa-

torial Africa. Less timid and more easily tamed, they are shown in zoos more often than is the Common Waterbuck. They may associate with Elands, Zebras, and Hartebeests.

LECHWES, or Lechwe's Waterbucks(3½ ft.), are antelopes that prefer swamps and grassy flats along rivers. Frequently feed on submerged vegetation. Large hoofs aid in getting through mud. Kobs, one of the several species in equatorial Africa, have shorter fur and horns.

Brindled Gnu

Blesbok

Hartebeest

GNUS, or Wildebeests, are noticeably higher at their shoulders (3–4 ft.) than at their hindquarters, as are Hartebeests. Both sexes have heavy, curved horns, conspicuous chin whiskers, a horselike tail, and a broad, sad-looking face. White-tailed Gnus have been nearly exterminated from the veld of South Africa but do well in zoos. Brindled Gnus are more numerous than the White-tailed.

BLESBOKS (3–4 ft. at shoulder), smaller relatives of Hartebeests, have a white face with a dark bar extending between the eyes.

Male's ringed horns are about 1½ ft. long; female's, shorter. Once widespread in South Africa but now live only in zoos and protected areas. Zoos have helped to preserve this species.

HARTEBEESTS (4–5 ft. at shoulder) are the most common antelopes of the African plains. They travel in small herds, often with zebras and gnus. They are fast but ungainly runners, using a lumbering, half-sideways gallop to depart an area when they sight or scent trouble. Hartebeests are rarely shown in large numbers in zoos.

DUIKERS are small African antelopes, varying from donkey-size to jackrabbit-size. Some kinds are reddish; others are blue-gray. Both sexes have spikelike horns. Duikers live in thick brush and escape predators by diving into the underbrush (duiker is Cape Dutch for "diver"). They usually travel alone or in twos and threes. Duikers are all shy, hence they are difficult to display in zoos.

KLIPSPRINGERS are rock-climbing, gazelle-like antelopes (p. 88) of tropical Africa. Only 20 in. high at the shoulder, their tiny hoofs provide sure-footedness, like that of the Chamois and the American Mountain Goat. They feed on plants and require little water. Few seen in zoos, as captives do poorly.

DIK-DIKS are small, weighing only 6 or 7 lbs. and standing 14 in. at the shoulders. Horns, present only in males, are short and point backward. A flexible nose projects beyond their lips. Dik-diks hide in thick African brush. Zoos rarely have Dik-diks to exhibit, as captive specimens are usually short-lived.

SPRINGBOKS (2½ ft. at shoulder), like gazelles and the Impala, are excellent jumpers. They make vertical leaps of as much as 10 ft. Springboks graze on open plains of South Africa where giant herds once made great migrations. Still the national emblem of the Union of South Africa. Springboks have been widely exterminated.

Gray Duiker

Klipspringer

Kirk's Dik-dik

Springbok

DORCAS GAZELLE, one of the fleet-footed, small (2 ft. at shoulders) antelopes, is found in deserts of North Africa, Syria, and Palestine. Gazelles forage on grass and leaves of desert plants, preferring open country where they can outrun predators. Most have black-and-white facial markings. In captivity, gazelles have less room to display their grace, speed, and jumping abilities. Dorcas Gazelles tame readily when the young are hand-reared. If the winters are cold, zoos provide heated quarters for these delicate antelopes.

GRANT'S GAZELLES (2½–3 ft. at shoulder) have the longest horns (to 30 in.) of all the gazelles. Both sexes have horns. Herds frequently congregate around water holes and sometimes wander into the sparse acacia forests. Gerenuks, or Waller's Gazelles, have an especially long neck and legs. In feeding, they stand on their hind legs and munch on choice but otherwise unobtainable tree leaves on twigs. The horns (males only) are heavily ringed. Both Grant's Gazelle and Gerenuks live in East Africa. Few are shown in zoos.

Gerenuk

Dorcas Gazelle

Grant's Gazelle

IMPALAS are noted for their jumping ability, as these 3 ft. animals often leap 8 ft. in the air and sometimes spring as far as 35 ft. They seem to jump for the fun of it. Once common in many parts of Africa, they now are seen principally in East Africa and in sanctuaries. Herds of as many as 100 may be found in the sparse bush country. Impalas are a favorite food of lions. Only males have horns (to over 30 in.). Most zoos have not been successful in establishing herds. Impalas usually live less than 4 yrs. in captivity.

THOMSON'S GAZELLES are the common small antelopes (2 ft. at shoulder) of Central Africa. Thousands of them can often be seen on the open plains. They can be recognized by their reddish upperparts separated from the white underparts by a conspicuous jet-black band. Known to many as "Tommy's," these gazelles have long been hunted by man and by many carnivores. Like other gazelles, they are excellent runners. "Tommy's" are probably the most common gazelles in zoos. In captivity they live less than 10 years.

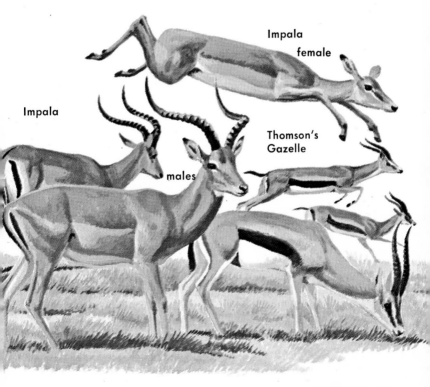

Impala female

Impala

Thomson's Gazelle

males

Gemsbok

Sable Antelope

Blackbuck

Saiga

GEMSBOKS (5½–6 ft. at shoulder) have straight horns, 4 ft. long. In equatorial South Africa, small herds often travel in a trot, single file. Closely related is the Beisa Oryx. Neither is common in U.S. zoos.

BLACKBUCKS (4 ft.) are Indian gazelles. Males have corkscrew-shaped horns. They live in small herds on the open plains where they have a better chance of escaping such enemies as the cheetah. In captivity, they eat hay, grain, and grasses.

SABLE ANTELOPES of equatorial Africa have long (5 ft.), curved horns. These 500 lb. animals are in many ways the most handsome of the antelopes. They are much sought after but are uncommon in most zoos.

SAIGAS (sigh'-gas) are gazelle-like antelopes (5 ft. at shoulder) of the Central Asian steppes. They have a bulbous, slightly pendant nose, short legs for such a thick body, heavily ringed horns. Zoos must learn more about diet to keep them successfully.

GIRAFFES, tallest of all animals, can browse on twigs and leaves more than 18 ft. above ground, far out of reach of other ground-dwelling animals. They pluck these leaves with a very long (up to 18 in.) tongue and mobile lips. To drink or to feed from the ground, a giraffe spreads its front legs far apart and bends down. Captives do well on a diet of hay, grain pellets, diced vegetables, and fruits. Giraffes are native to Central and South Africa where they live in small herds. When they run, both legs on the same side swing in tandem, giving the giraffe a rolling gait. Giraffes are nearly mute but can grunt or whimper and also produce a whistle-like sound.

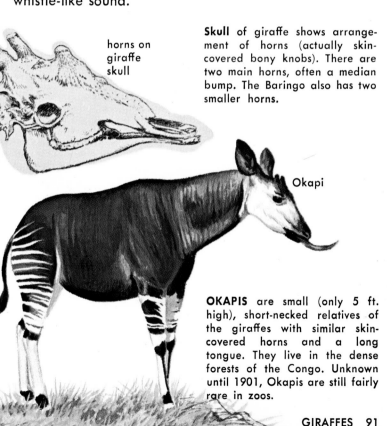

horns on giraffe skull

Skull of giraffe shows arrangement of horns (actually skin-covered bony knobs). There are two main horns, often a median bump. The Baringo also has two smaller horns.

Okapi

OKAPIS are small (only 5 ft. high), short-necked relatives of the giraffes with similar skin-covered horns and a long tongue. They live in the dense forests of the Congo. Unknown until 1901, Okapis are still fairly rare in zoos.

GIRAFFES (8–12 ft. at shoulder) in different parts of Africa vary in color and pattern, but there are overlaps in these features. Nubian Giraffes are spotted. Masai Giraffes have irregular, leaf-like spots.

Nubian
Giraffe

Masai
Giraffe

Reticulated Giraffes have a network (reticulation) of light-colored lines dividing a dark-brown coat. The reticulation is less pronounced and the legs are a lighter color in Baringo Giraffes. Distinctive coat patterns are lost when there is interbreeding of the different kinds of giraffes.

Reticulated
Giraffe

Baringo
Giraffe

93

Rock Hyrax

HYRAXES, also called Conies or Dassies, are rabbit-sized hoofed mammals with even-toed forefeet and odd-toed hind feet. Although distantly related to elephants and horses, they behave more like small goats, easily climbing rocky cliffs and even trees. Hyraxes are found in Africa and Syria.

ODD-TOED hoofed mammals (Perissodactyla) carry most of their weight on one toe (their third) and do not chew a cud. Included are tapirs, horses, and rhinos.

TAPIRS look much like miniature elephants or overgrown pigs. Adults may reach 8 ft. in length and weigh 500 lbs. The nose extends beyond the mouth in a short proboscis. In captivity, they can be fed hay, grains, and given vegetables with vitamin supplements. Keepers find they usually are docile.

SOUTH AMERICAN TAPIRS do well in many zoos but in cold weather need heated quarters. Young are spotted and striped.

MALAYAN TAPIRS of southern and peninsular Asia are becoming scarce. Zoos are an important sanctuary for this species.

Malayan Tapir

South American Tapir

Onager

HORSES belong to a family containing a single genus, *Equus*. It includes asses and zebras as well as the familiar domestic horse.

ONAGERS (above) are wild asses of Central Asia. They have short ears and a long tail without much hair. Adult males seldom weigh more than 500 lbs. The closely related Kiang of Tibet and Nepal is sometimes shown in zoos. Wild asses of Africa are smaller but have larger ears. Like their Asiatic relatives, they have a short, stiff mane. Domestic donkeys are descendants of African species.

PRZEWALSKI'S HORSE (about 4 ft. at the shoulder) is stockily built, with a black, erect mane and a long-haired tail. Its legs are black to the knees, and the summer coat shows a black stripe down the back. A few of these never-domesticated horses live wild in remote parts of the Gobi Desert. Captives and their offspring are so rare that all of them (about 100) are listed in a special stud book.

Przewalski's Horse

95

Grevy's Zebra

foal

ZEBRAS (4–4½ ft. at shoulder) are white horses with black stripes and erect manes. The stripes serve as camouflage on the grassy African plains. Foals have same markings as adults. Often attacked by lions, zebras defend themselves by kicking and biting. Hunted also by man, zebras are becoming scarce except in parks and sanctuaries. In captivity, they need rubbing posts and rolling pits to keep trim. Cannot tolerate cold.

GREVY'S ZEBRA is one of the three species of zebras. Size and pattern of the stripes are useful in distinguishing the different kinds. Grevy's has narrow stripes extending down to its hoofs, a white belly, large ears, and spinal stripe extending onto the tail. Zoo diet is hay and oats, plus diced vegetables and salt.

Chapman's Zebra
a form of Burchell's

Grant's Zebra
a form of Burchell's

Mountain
Zebra

BURCHELL'S ZEBRAS are of several varieties: Grant's (with bold, contrasting stripes), Chapman's (with brownish stripes between the black ones), Burchell's proper (with no markings on the lower legs). Although sometimes displayed in large enclosures with antelopes, stallion zebras may bother other animals.

MOUNTAIN ZEBRAS, a distinct species of South Africa, are smaller than other zebras and have a small fold of skin (dewlap) on the throat. Broad stripes mark the flanks and band the legs to the hoofs. Mountain Zebras have been exterminated in some areas and are uncommon in protected areas and in zoos.

RHINOCEROSES are thick-skinned, nearly hairless animals of large size (shoulder height, to 6½ ft.; weight, to 4,500 lbs.). Their one or two horns are not true bony outgrowths; they consist of hardened and compressed hairlike fibers on a bony base at the front of the skull. These continue to grow throughout the life of the animal. In the wild, rhinos may be bad-tempered, but captives usually are fairly docile. When annoyed, a lone rhinoceros may attack a train or a car, charging at speeds to 30 miles per hour. Zoos keep them in moated outdoor cages and heated indoor winter quarters.

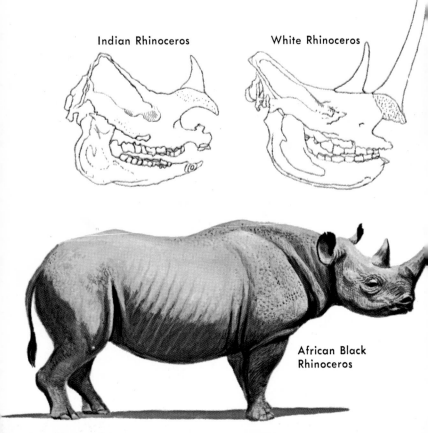

Indian Rhinoceros

White Rhinoceros

African Black Rhinoceros

AFRICAN BLACK RHINOCEROSES (11 ft. long; 5½ ft. at shoulder) have two horns, the front one larger and, if intact, up to 50 in. long. The hide is dark brown, not black. Sometimes they are called Hook-lipped Rhinos because of their peculiarly shaped upper lip, adapted for grasping twigs and leaves. They live in thorn country throughout much of Africa. Most zoos show the Black Rhino, which is the most numerous of the five recognized species of rhinos.

INDIAN RHINOCEROSES are one-horned and large (14 ft. long). The leathery skin is separated into plates by deep folds and is covered with hard knobs. Only a few, perhaps no more than 600, remain in India, Assam, and Nepal.

WHITE RHINOCEROSES, also called Square-lipped Rhinos, are two-horned, plains dwellers of equatorial Africa. They may be 14 ft. long, 6½ ft. at shoulders. Rarely displayed in zoos.

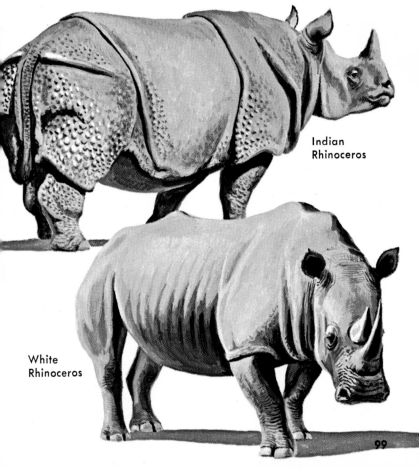

Indian
Rhinoceros

White
Rhinoceros

ELEPHANTS, the largest living land animals, may eat a quarter of a ton of forage a day. Food includes leaves, roots, fruits and, in captivity, hay and grain. The elephant's trunk is its nose, a double-tubed flexible proboscis with nostrils at the end. Water and even food can be snuffed part way up

ASIAN ELEPHANTS are often called Indian Elephants. Found in the Oriental region, south of the Himalayas from Burma and India to Sumatra, they live in slightly hilly forests, particularly those with much bamboo—a favorite food. Males weigh up to 6 tons, stand about 10 ft. tall, and have small ears. Commonly trained as work animals.

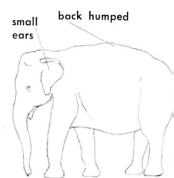

small ears

back humped

Asian Elephant

single finger

the proboscis and blown into the mouth. Tusks, larger in males, are modified upper incisor teeth. Usually a single woolly young is born, weighing about 200 lbs. It soon becomes nearly hairless. A daily hosing and a massage with a stiff broom keeps an elephant's skin in good condition.

AFRICAN ELEPHANTS have large ears and tusks. Males weigh up to 7 tons. Found south of the Sahara Desert in Africa, they are of two varieties: Bush Elephants, with males that may stand 11 ft. tall at the shoulders; and Forest Elephants, the males to 8 ft. tall. Pygmy Elephants usually are young Forest Elephants; they are not a distinct kind.

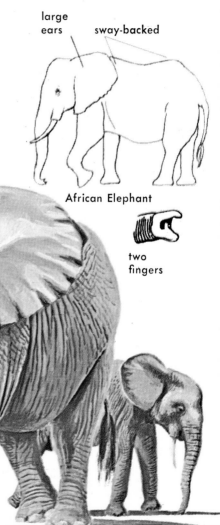

large ears   sway-backed

African Elephant

two fingers

Giant flight cage at the National Zoo in Washington, D.C.

BIRDS

Birds are the only animals with feathers. Most of the more than 8,500 species are efficient fliers. Hollow or spongy bones, enlarged breast muscles to move the wings, and long, strong wing feathers enable birds to fly. A few kinds can fly faster than 100 m.p.h., and many can travel great distances without resting. Birds lay hard-shelled eggs, usually in some kind of nest.

Many zoos feature spacious flyways, or flight cages, that can house 100 or more birds. The captives can exercise freely, and some even mate, build nests, and raise young. In some zoos, visitors can enter the flyways and mingle with the birds in the open.

FLIGHTLESS (RATITE) BIRDS belonging to several groups, or orders, share the loss of ability to fly. All have a flat rather than raised, or keeled, breastbone for attachment of powerful flight muscles. Their wings are small and useless, but their legs are strong for running. In these birds, males incubate the eggs, with the exception of some Ostriches.

OSTRICHES are the largest (to 8 ft. tall and more than 300 lbs.) of all living birds. Their eggs may weigh as much as 3 lbs. and are incubated for about 40 days. Birds mature in 3 to 4 years. Males are black, with white wing tips and tail plumes; females, brownish. Ostriches travel across Central African deserts in bands of up to 50, often with herds of zebras and antelopes. When threatened, an Ostrich will run—as fast as 30 m.p.h. Ostriches in captivity will hiss and kick. They do well in zoos, where some have lived for more than 25 years.

Ostrich

male

female

CASSOWARIES, about 5 ft. tall, are shy forest-dwellers of northern Australia and New Guinea. A ridged, bony "helmet" covers their forehead, and long quills on their small wings stick out beyond their body feathers. Their normal diet is fruit, but they may also hunt rodents.

KIWIS (2 ft. tall) live in the forests of New Zealand. Rarely seen in the wild and displayed in only a few zoos outside their native country, where they are the national emblem. Their nostrils are at the tip of their 6 in. bill with which they probe in soft dirt and leaves for worms.

RHEAS stand 4 to 5 ft. tall but weigh only about 50 lbs. Often called American ostriches, they live in the grasslands and brushlands of South America. They have softer feathers than the Ostrich, have three toes instead of two, and lack tail plumes. In captivity they become tame.

EMUS live in the deserts and grasslands of Australia. About 6 ft. tall and weighing up to 120 lbs., they rank second to the Ostrich in size. The friendliest of the flightless birds, Emus often graze with cattle or with kangaroos. The eggs, 7 to 12 in a clutch, are greenish black.

PENGUINS are swimming birds that live in the coastal waters of the Southern Hemisphere, including Antarctica. One species, the Galapagos Penguin, lives on Pacific islands as far north as the equator. Their flipper-like nearly featherless wings propel them through the water as fast as 25 m.p.h.

EMPEROR PENGUINS, largest of the penguins, stand 4 ft. tall. They spend most of their life at sea off Antarctica, coming ashore only to reproduce. The female lays a single egg, which the male holds on his feet and incubates by pressing it into a fold of skin on his belly. Later the female returns from sea to help feed the chick. The King Penguin is the only other that makes no nest.

KING PENGUINS, about 3½ ft. tall, live on islands near Antarctica, sometimes appearing off New Zealand and South America. In zoos, they must be hand fed; other penguins will eat fish from pools or from the ground.

HUMBOLDT PENGUINS, less than 2 ft. tall, lay two eggs in a nest. Live on islands off the west coast of South America, north to Peru.

Emperor Penguin

King Penguin

Humboldt Penguin

Shag

Great Cormorant

Brown Pelican

Anhin[ga]

European White Pelican

FISH-EATING BIRDS have broad wings, long bills, and are good fliers. Most can swim well, but they have short legs and walk clumsily on land. Their four toes are connected by webs, and they have a throat pouch, most highly developed in pelicans.

CORMORANTS, or Shags, live along coastal waters, lakes, and rivers all over the world. They dive and then swim underwater to catch fish. Wingspan about 5 ft. Bones are heavier than those of pelicans, hence birds sink quickly. Often swim with only head and neck above surface.

WHITE PELICANS have a wingspan of about 9 ft. One species lives in the New World; another in the Old World. White Pelicans nest on inland lakes. Several birds work together to herd fish into the shallows to catch them. They do not dive.

BROWN PELICANS have a wingspan of more than 6 ft. They soar 10 to 30 ft. over the sea, then dive straight down to scoop up a fish. Their pouch can hold two gallons of water. Captives eat fish, meat scraps, and mice. Brown Pelicans are found only in the Americas.

ANHINGAS, or Snakebirds, have a long, slim neck, small head, and pointed bill. Wingspan about 4 ft. They spear fish with their bill while swimming underwater. Quickly become watersoaked, hence often seen with wings spread to dry in sun.

WADING BIRDS (herons and their allies) have long legs, neck, and bill. Their tail is short, their wings broad. Most are fish-eaters. In zoos, storks are hesitant eaters and may not get their share of food.

SHOEBILL STORKS, or Whaleheads, stand about 4 ft. tall. Their bills, 8 in. long and nearly as wide, are used to probe in the mud for food. They are native to the swampy lowlands of the Upper Nile River of Africa.

SADDLE-BILLED STORKS, from tropical Africa, stand nearly 4½ ft. tall. They have a yellow, saddle-shaped shield on top of their long, red-and-black bill.

JABIRUS, tallest (4½ ft.) of the American storks, are found from Mexico to Argentina. The bird's featherless, blue-black neck has a red or orange base. Adults have white plumage; the young are brownish.

Jabiru

Shoebill
Stork

Saddle-billed
Stork

Great Blue Heron

White Stork

Wood Stork

Common Egret

GREAT BLUE HERONS, of North America, stand about 4½ ft. tall. They frequently are called "cranes." Imperial and Giant herons of Asia and Africa are similar in size and equally handsome. All herons have long, sharp bills.

COMMON EGRETS, about 3 ft. tall, are all-white herons of warm regions throughout the world. The one found in the New World is called American Egret. They stalk insects, frogs, and fishes in shallows or marshes.

WHITE STORKS winter in Africa and nest in the summer on rooftops in Europe, where they are considered a good-luck omen. These tall (3½ ft.) white birds have black wing feathers and a red bill and legs. White Storks are becoming scarce.

WOOD STORKS, or Wood Ibises (4 ft. tall), are found from southern United States to northern South America. Live in colonies and build large nests high in trees in marshes. Several dozen may build in same tree.

Roseate Spoonbill

Greater Flamingo

Scarlet Ibis

ROSEATE SPOONBILLS, found only in the Americas, scoop up food by swinging opened bill back and forth in shallow water. Near tip, spoon-shaped bill is broader than the bird's head. Eurasian Spoonbill is similar in size (3 ft.), has a shaggy mane.

SCARLET IBISES (2 ft. tall) are native to South America, where great numbers have been killed for their feathers. Strays north to southern U.S. Ibises have a thin, down-curved bill used to catch insects and crustaceans.

GREATER FLAMINGOS (about 4 ft. tall) live in subtropical regions. They invert their head to sieve food from muddy waters through their bent-down, flat-topped bill. To preserve their bright color in captivity, they are fed a mix of carrot juice, paprika, boiled beets, and raw shrimp. The same is fed to spoonbills and ibises. Without this, their color fades to a washed-out pink. Flamingos build mud nests 2 ft. or more tall and lay their single egg in the shallow depression on its top.

SWANS, GEESE, AND DUCKS typically have a long neck and a short, flat bill. Their legs are short and their feet webbed for swimming. Ducks and swans feed by dabbling or diving. Geese forage mainly on land, eating grasses and roots. In zoos, these waterfowl are fed pellets of laying hen feed and "greens."

MUTE SWANS, pure white with a black knob on their bill, are native to Europe and Asia but have been introduced to North America and Australia, where some have gone wild. An albino form is common. Mute Swans can hiss and make feeble "barking" sounds. Wingspan, 5 ft.

BLACK SWANS can trumpet. They have white wing feathers that show only when the birds are in flight. Black Swans are native to Australia and Tasmania. They are raised in captivity, however, and have been introduced into New Zealand and other regions.

BLACK-NECKED SWANS, of southern South America and the Falkland Islands, are smaller than other swans. The black neck and red bill are distinctive.

Mute Swan
60 in.

Black-necked Swan
42 in.

Black Swan
56-60 in.

CANADA GEESE, the largest North American goose, weigh as much as 13½ lbs. In spring, large flocks migrate to northern nesting grounds, making loud honking sounds as they fly. Unlike ducks, both males and females have same coloring.

RED-BREASTED GEESE are brightly colored, small geese that nest in the Siberian tundra and winter near the Caspian Sea. Barnacle Geese of northern Europe are closely related to the Red-breasted Goose. Both are related to the Canada Goose.

BLACK-NECKED SCREAMERS of South America are swan-sized, aquatic birds. Day and night they honk noisily. Air cells between skin and body give them unusual buoyancy. Each wing has two well-developed spurs, which can inflict painful wounds.

TREE DUCKS, or Whistling Ducks, have gooselike posture, perch in trees near water, and feed in nearby fields. All have a squealing whistle. The pink-billed Black-bellied Tree Duck (wingspan, 3 ft.) ranges from southern Texas to northern Argentina.

Canada Goose
22-43 in.

Black-necked
Screamer
28 in.

Black-bellied
Tree Duck

Red-breasted
Goose   22 in.

MANDARIN DUCKS, from Asia and Japan, spend more time in trees than do most ducks, even nesting in tree holes. Both sexes have long feathers on back of head. Wood Ducks, closely related, also nest in tree holes. Wingspan of both about 2 ft.

COMMON SHELDUCKS (wingspan, 3 ft.) are gooselike ducks of Eurasia. Males have a large knob on their red bill. Shelducks lay smooth eggs in nests in underground burrows. Other species in Africa and Australia are sometimes called Sheldrakes.

SHOVELERS are dabbling ducks with large spoon-shaped bills. They feed in shallows using the comblike teeth on edges of bill to strain tiny plants, seeds, and crustaceans from water. Females: mottled brown with blue on wings. Wingspan, 2½ ft.

MALLARDS (wingspan, 3 ft.) are Northern Hemisphere, river-and-pond ducks that feed by "tipping up" to pull plants and mollusks from under the water. Usually nest on dry ground near water. Blue wing patches bordered with white identify them.

Common Shelduck

Mandarin Duck

Mallard

Wood Duck

Shoveler

DIURNAL BIRDS OF PREY include hawks, eagles, and other flesh-eating hunters with hooked bills and sharp talons. Vultures are included but are mainly carrion eaters. In zoos, these birds are fed a vitamin-sprinkled, protein diet. Keepers often must force these birds to exercise to keep them lean.

LAMMERGEYER, or Bearded Vulture, with beadlike bristles beneath the bill, carry bones cleaned of flesh by other animals high into the air, then drop them onto rocks, and extract and eat the marrow. This 4 ft. kite lives in the Old World.

KING VULTURES, found from Mexico to Argentina, are about 2½ ft. long. They have a colorful, featherless head and neck. Like other vultures, they are excellent soarers. King Vultures are sociable with cage mates except at feeding time.

SECRETARY BIRDS, from Africa, eat small animals, including snakes which they stamp on to keep them from coiling and wriggling. Nearly 4 ft. tall and with penlike quills behind their head, they can walk faster than a man can run.

Lammergeyer

King
Vulture

Secretary
Bird

Bald
Eagle

BALD EAGLES, national emblem of the United States, are not bald, but the white feathers on the adult's head and neck give them a bald appearance. Males have a wingspread of nearly 8 ft. Bald Eagles build huge stick nests high in dead trees or on rock ledges. The female lays 2 or 3 eggs. The young are a streaked brown and do not develop adult plumage for 3 years. Bald Eagles live in North America and northeastern Asia, but are becoming exceedingly rare. Most abundant in Alaska.

Harpy Eagle

HARPY EAGLES, about the same size as the Bald Eagle, catch monkeys, parrots, and sloths in tropical forests of Central and South America. In captivity, sleep all day; active at night.

BATALEUR EAGLES, smaller and with short tail and broad wings, are skillful acrobats and excellent soarers. They hunt the grasslands and open forests of Africa, swooping down from high in the air to prey on small game, snakes, or locusts.

Bataleur
Eagle   24 in.

Peregrine Falcon

Caracara

Red-tailed Hawk

PEREGRINE FALCONS, or Duck Hawks, dive on flying ducks or other birds at a speed as great as 175 m.p.h. They strike with their feet, causing the prey to fall to earth where the falcon then retrieves them. They have been trained as hunting "hawks." Peregrine Falcons (wingspan about 3 ft.) are found along cliffs near water throughout the world but are nowhere abundant. Falcons have long, pointed wings, lower legs free of feathers, and a notch or tooth in the upper bill. The Sparrow Hawk is a common falcon found throughout the Americas.

CARACARAS are falcons that feed in flocks, primarily on carcasses of dead animals as vultures do. Audubon's Caracara, national bird of Mexico, and several other kinds are found from southern United States to central South America. Wingspan to 4 ft.

RED-TAILED HAWKS, found from Alaska to Panama, are large, slow-flying hawks that feed mainly on rodents and rabbits. With broad wings (span to 4 ft.) and a short, round tail, they can soar, like vultures, but spend most of their time perched.

FOWL-LIKE BIRDS, all much like chickens in their habits, have stout legs and strong feet with which they scratch on the ground to find their food. They can run fast and can also fly—but only for short distances. All have a thick, down-curved bill.

PEAFOWL are native to India and Ceylon but well known throughout the world. Males are peacocks; females, peahens. Commonly given free run in zoos. Males lift train of long, spotted upper tail feathers and spread them as a fan in courting displays. To 7 ft. long, including the handsome tail.

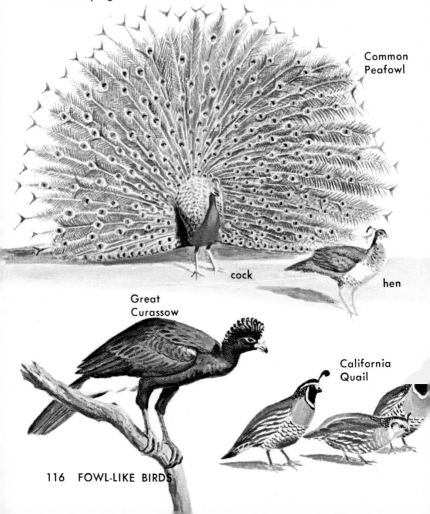

Common Peafowl

cock

hen

Great Curassow

California Quail

GREAT CURASSOW is a turkey-sized forest dweller from southern Mexico to Ecuador. Curassows usually stay in trees and run agilely along the branches. Like other curassows, all easily tamed, the Great Curassow has a feathered crest. Males have a fleshy knob on top of bill.

QUAIL and partridges, found throughout the world, are small chicken-like birds closely related to pheasants. Males of several species have conspicuous head plumes. Where succulent plants are available, some quail can do without water for months.

PHEASANTS (about 2½ ft. long) are native to Asia but have been introduced to most parts of world. Males have gaudy plumage and a long, pointed or arched tail. Brownish female has a shorter tail. Golden Pheasants are common in zoos but almost extinct in their native China. Silver Pheasants, from mountainous southeastern Asia, are silvery white with black underparts. Tragopans are short-tailed pheasants of the Himalayas. Males have two large hornlike wattles under a crown of feathers. Other colorful pheasants are also kept in zoos.

Golden Pheasant

Temminck's Tragopan

Silver Pheasant

CRANES are long-legged birds, and their bill is usually longer than their head. In flight, the neck is held straight rather than crooked as in herons. Captive cranes are kept from flying by wing clipping, but they still jump fences. Bustards are closely related to cranes.

CROWNED CRANES (3 ft. tall) have powerful, booming voices. The handsome crown is thin but stiff and strawlike in adults; smaller and not well formed in the young. They eat insects and reptiles and have been tamed and kept in gardens for this purpose. Native to Africa, they live in marshy areas and build bulky nests on ground. Becoming rare where wetlands are drained.

SARUS CRANES (about 5 ft. tall) range from India to Philippines. Pairs mate for life, as do other cranes. All also perform dances.

GREAT BUSTARDS, shorter legged than other cranes, are among the heaviest of flying birds. Males weigh 25 to 35 lbs.; females, 11 to 13 lbs. Great Bustards have been exterminated in most of Eurasia.

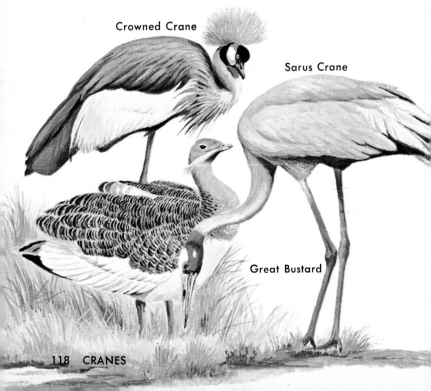

Crowned Crane

Sarus Crane

Great Bustard

SHOREBIRDS are long-legged, web-footed ground nesters that live in marshes or along shores. They eat a variety of small animals.

BLACK-NECKED STILTS are small (14 in.) wading birds with long, stiltlike legs. They probe in mud with slender bills for food. Build nests on marshy ground. They live in North America and northern South America.

CROCODILE BIRDS, or Black-backed Coursers (9 in.), live on sandy banks of Africa's rivers. Reputedly, though not authenticated, they enter crocodiles' mouths for food. These birds generally bury their eggs in moist sand where they are incubated by the sun's heat.

LEAST SANDPIPERS are 6 in. birds that are found along coastal mud flats of North America. There are many kinds of sandpipers and any of several may be displayed in zoos as available. In the wild, sandpipers forage for food in large flocks.

GULLS (more than 40 species) live along coastal areas throughout the world. The closely related terns are smaller and more graceful fliers. Gulls eat mostly dead fish and other carrion; terns eat mostly live fish. Herring Gulls (wingspan nearly 5 ft.) are found along the coasts and some inland waterways in Northern Hemisphere. Laughing Gulls, named for unusual call, occur on both coasts of the Americas. Many kinds of gulls are shown in zoos.

Black-necked Stilt

Crocodile Bird

Least Sandpiper

Herring Gull

Laughing Gull

Magnificant Fruit Pigeon

Bleeding Heart Pigeon

Ground Dove

PIGEONS AND DOVES are members of the same family. Doves are small and graceful; pigeons are chunkier. Both generally make cooing sounds, and unlike other birds, they drink by sucking water up through the bill. Parents feed the young "pigeon's milk" which is composed of fat cells from the lining of the crop.

FRUIT PIGEONS (14 in.) are brightly colored tropical forest dwellers of the Old World. They feed on fruits and berries, rarely coming to the ground.

BLEEDING HEART PIGEONS (12 in.) have a bright red splash, resembling blood, on an otherwise all white breast.

GROUND DOVES (7 in.), slightly larger than sparrows, inhabit warmer parts of America. Tail is short and broad.

CROWNED PIGEONS, 3 ft. long, are the largest and most spectacular of the pigeons. These New Guinea birds have a lacy crown of head feathers and have been hunted for plumes.

MOURNING DOVES (12 in.) are found from Canada to Mexico. They live close to human habitations and have a soft cooing call. Hunting regulations make it less likely that these birds will become extinct as did Passenger Pigeon, which they resemble.

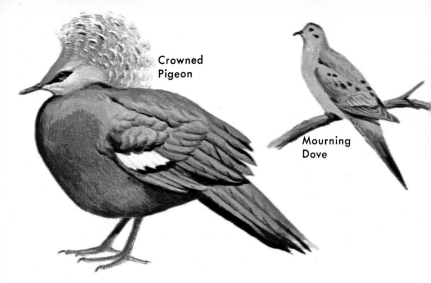

Crowned Pigeon

Mourning Dove

TOURACOS, Africa, have a unique coppery-red pigment (turacin) on their wings. It is said to be water-soluble. Touracos are also called Plantain (banana) Eaters but appear to like berries and seeds best. They glide from tree to tree and run along the branches like squirrels in search of food.

GO-AWAY BIRDS, touracos of savannas and forests of east-central Africa, reportedly follow hunters and frighten off quarry by crying "Go-away." Largest touraco is the Blue, 3 ft. long.

Go-Away Bird

Knysna Touraco

Sulfur-crested Cockatoo

PARROTS AND THEIR ALLIES have a large head, hooked bill, and heavy legs and feet. They use the bill as a nutcracker or rasp, moving the lower against the upper. Their feet are used for climbing or to hold food. Many can learn to imitate the human voice, some kinds better than others. Their gaudy colors, clownlike behavior, and mimicking voices have endeared them as pets since ancient times. Cockatoos have crests and short tail feathers, Macaws have a long tail, no crest. Parakeets and lorikeets are long-tailed and slim bodied.

SCARLET MACAWS (36 in.), native to tropical America, are hardy, long-lived, vividly colored, and popular pets. Trained to talk, these parrots can make a wide range of soft sounds, though their natural voice is harsh. They are playful; need wood to shred to keep bill trim.

GOLD-AND-BLUE MACAWS (30 in.), from northern South America, are alert, intelligent, sharp-voiced mimics. Active fliers, these birds must be given plenty of room to exercise in captivity.

SULFUR - CRESTED COCKATOOS (18 in.) are loud, hardy Australian birds. These handsome birds are known to live to 30 years.

AFRICAN GRAY PARROTS (12–15 in.) live in the Congo and Gold Coast rain forests. Their voices sound very human, and they are considered the best talkers. In captivity, they may live for more than 50 years. In the wild, roost in flocks or in pairs; destructive to grain fields.

YELLOW-HEADED AMAZONS (15 in.) are one of many so-called Amazon parrots found from Mexico to South America. All are greenish. The Yellow-headed is a good talker, if trained young.

COCKATIELS (15 in.), from Australia, are gentle and affectionate. They are fair talkers and good whistlers, easy to care for.

Scarlet
Macaw

Gold-and-Blue
Macaw

Yellow-headed
Amazon

African Gray
Parrot

Cockatiel

BUDGERIGARS, of Australia, are known also as Budgies, Shell Parakeets, and even as Australian Lovebirds. Through selective breeding, many varieties have been developed. Some are predominantly blue, others yellow, yellowish-green, cobalt, even albino. In the wild, they live in colonies. They feed on all kinds of small seeds, lay up to nine eggs, and sometimes raise two broods in a year. Their notes are a buzzing whistle or a warble. Trained budgies can whistle a tune. Budgies are common pets throughout world. About 7 in. long.

Orange-chinned Parakeet

LORIKEETS crush flowers for nectar and juice, which they lap up as cats do milk. Their tongue is brushlike at the tip. Lorikeets live in the Australasian jungles. One of the most colorful is the Rainbow Lorikeet (10 in.). May be fed sugar water or honey.

PARAKEETS, from Southeast Asia, are small (about 8 in.) parrots with a pointed tail. Largest is the Indian Ring-necked (16 in.), a popular cage bird since Roman times. Most of the many kinds live in large flocks and feed on the ground. Members of one group feed and sleep hanging upside down from branches.

Rainbow Lorikeet

LOVEBIRDS, miniature (5 in.) parrots of Africa, have been tamed for centuries and are found in captivity throughout the world. Pairs of Lovebirds may show great attachment, sitting for hours bill to bill. The call note is shrill and strong.

Budgerigar

Barred Parakeet

Long-tailed Parakeet

Indian Ring-necked Parakeet

Masked Lovebirds

FROGMOUTHS, related to nighthawks and whip-poor-wills, live in forests of Australia and eastern Asia. Unlike nighthawks, frogmouths catch their food — beetles, scorpions, caterpillars, and even mice — on the ground. Call is a low booming.

Tawny Frogmouth 18 in.

OWLS are nocturnal birds of prey that live in all parts of the world except Antarctica. Their silent flight is due to their soft plumage. Keen hearing and sight, and sharp, curved claws enable them to seize rodents, insects, birds, even fish in darkness. Owls swallow prey whole and later regurgitate undigested pellets of feathers, fur, and bone. Calls range from hoots to screeches and sounds like snores and coughs.

Malay Fishing Owl 24 in.

Snowy Owl 20 in.

Barn Owl 14 in.

FISHING OWLS of several species are found in Asia and Africa. They roost in trees along streams to prey on fish, frogs, and crabs. They also eat small mammals.

BARN OWLS, also called Monkey-faced Owls, have a heart-shaped ring of feathers around the eyes. Their young are often raised in deserted barns or attics. Calls are screeches and squeaks.

SNOWY OWLS, of the Arctic, can be displayed best in zoos because they are more active in daytime than other large owls. Females are larger and more powerful than males. Their light color matches snowy habitat.

TROGONS live in the tropical rain forests of Asia, Africa, and the Americas. Males are colorful; the females less striking. All are sluggish, poor fliers. They are mainly insect eaters, though some eat fruit. The ornate Quetzal (p. 3), national emblem of Guatemala, is most handsome of trogons.

Bar-tailed Trogon 10 in.

HUMMINGBIRDS, the smallest of all birds, beat their wings so rapidly that they actually make a humming noise. They can fly forward, backward, sideways. To feed, they hover over a flower, insert their bill, and suck up nectar. In captivity, they are given a mix of honey or sugar and water, fruit flies, and condensed milk. Males are more brightly colored than females. About 300 species, all New World, found mostly in the tropics.

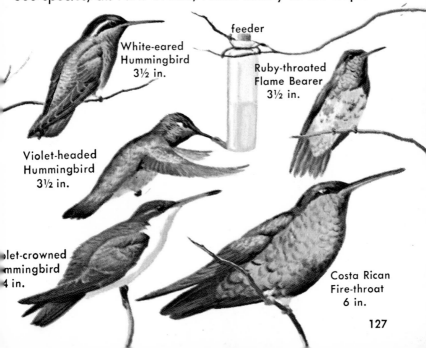

White-eared Hummingbird 3½ in.

feeder

Ruby-throated Flame Bearer 3½ in.

Violet-headed Hummingbird 3½ in.

Violet-crowned Hummingbird 4 in.

Costa Rican Fire-throat 6 in.

127

KINGFISHERS AND THEIR ALLIES are found throughout the world but mainly in the tropics and subtropics. All are stocky birds with a stout bill. Some live in the forests and eat insects and rodents. Others live near water and are mainly fish eaters.

MOTMOTS are jay-sized birds. Most have racket-shaped tail feathers kept trim and partially bare by constant preening. They feed on insects, lizards, and fruit. Motmots live in the lowland forests of the New World tropics.

HORNBILLS are from India and southeastern Asia. Mates select a hollow in a tree, and the cavity is sealed with mud to imprison the female. The male feeds her through a slit opening until after the chicks hatch.

KINGFISHERS have large heads and short tails. Belted Kingfishers, of North America, have a thin, pointed bill and feed mainly on fish. The Australian Kookaburra, or Laughing Jackass (because of fiendish calls), is a forest kingfisher, which have broader bills and feed on insects, lizards, and other land animals.

Turquoise-browed Motmot 13 in.

Great Hornbill 60 in.

Kookaburra 18 in.

Belted Kingfisher 12 in.

WOODPECKERS AND ALLIES are found mainly in the tropics throughout the world (except Australia); some live in colder climates. They nest in holes chiseled into trees or dug in the ground, are mainly insect eaters, and typically have two toes in front, two behind.

BARBETS are colorful, stocky birds with bristles around their bill. They live in the dry bush country and along the edges of tropical forests. Barbets are very noisy, some kinds repeating their "tinny" calls for hours.

Black-collared Barbet Africa 7½ in.

Toco Toucan Northern S.A. 25 in.

TOUCANS use their canoe shaped bills, half the length of their body, to skin fruit (their principal food), drill wood, probe in the mud, or tear flesh. When it sleeps, a toucan turns its head so that its long bill rests on its back, then folds its long tail neatly over it.

WOODPECKERS probe with their long, barbed tongue to get grubs, ants, other insects from the holes they drill. In captivity, they are fed a substitute diet of chopped eggs and horse meat. Red-headed Woodpeckers and sapsuckers feed in trees; flickers, mostly on the ground. Various woodpeckers may be displayed in zoos, depending on their availability.

Red-headed Woodpecker N.A. 10 in.

Yellow-shafted Flicker N.A. 12 in.

PERCHING BIRDS make up about three-fifths of the world's living bird population. Small to medium-sized, all are land birds. When a perching bird "squats" on a branch, tendons in each foot tighten its toes around the perch. They are loosened only when the bird stands up. Many kinds of perching birds are displayed in zoos; a few of the most colorful are shown here.

Red-breasted Blackbird S.A.

7½ in.

Chestnut-headed Oropendola Mex., S.A.

14 in.

BLACKBIRDS total more than 90 species, all American. Grackles, orioles, cowbirds, and meadowlarks are included in the group. Most blackbirds are omnivorous, but Oropendolas and other orioles of the American tropics are fruit eaters. Orioles build elaborate hanging nests. The Oropendolas may be 6 ft. long.

CROWS AND JAYS are a cosmopolitan group of about 100 species, including the magpies and the raven, largest of the perching birds. All are omnivorous, and most have harsh calls. They are among the most clever of the birds.

Troupial Northern S.A.

10 in.

18 in.

Formosan Red-billed Magpie Southeast Asia

Black-billed Magpie Western N.A.

18 in.

in.

Silver-beaked Tanager S.A.

7½ in.

Blue Tanager Cent. and S.A.

9 in.

Kiskadee Flycatcher Tex. to Brazil

TANAGERS are colorful, small New World birds of over 200 species. Most are poor singers. They prefer fruits and insects. Most tanagers build shallow nests, in a tree or a bush.

FLYCATCHERS use their broad bill to seize insects while in flight. The 365 species, all of the New World, are noise-makers rather than true songbirds. Includes kingbirds and phoebes.

STARLINGS of some 100 species live in Europe, Asia, and Africa. They were introduced into the U.S. Mynas whistle and imitate sounds. Wattled Starlings shed head feathers, grow fleshy wattles in breeding season. Superb Starling is shiny, metallic.

Wattled Starling Africa

12 in.

Superb Starling Africa in.

Hill Myna Southern Asia 12 in.

PERCHING BIRDS 131

Red-whiskered
Bulbul   8 in.

Pekin Robin
6 in.

BULBULS are chattering, singing birds from the tropical and sub-tropical forests of Africa to the Philippines. The Red-whiskered Bulbul, of southeastern Asia, prefers living in or near towns.

BABBLERS and their allies are all Old World species (except possibly the Wrentit of western U.S.). Their noisy chatter gives them their name. The Pekin Robin is one of the best singers.

COTINGAS AND MANAKINS include the colorful cocks-of-the-rock, bellbirds, and umbrellabirds. Females are usually drab. All are forest inhabitants of tropical America.

FINCHES AND SPARROWS (about 300 species) are mostly small birds, found mainly in the Americas. Included are grosbeaks, buntings, cardinals, and the many kinds of sparrows.

Cock-of-the-rock

Andean
Cock-of-the-rock

12 in.

Saffron
Finch
S.A.

5½ in.

Cardinal   8 in.
Eastern U.S., Mex

WEAVERBIRDS AND OLD WORLD SEED EATERS (about 300 species) include goldfinches, waxbills, and weaverbirds. Most chirp rather than sing, and many are colonial nesters. All are small, but some members of this group have long tail feathers.

Diamond Finch
Australia

5 in.

Chestnut
Mannikin
Southeastern
Asia

5 in.

6 in.

Gouldian
Finch   Northern Australia

5½ in.

Red Bishop
South Africa

Red-cheeked
Cordon-bleu
Africa

4½ in.

Great Bird
of Paradise

Satin
Bowerbird

BIRDS OF PARADISE (18 in.), relatives of the crows, inhabit the forests of New Guinea and neighboring areas. All the males have brightly colored plumage. Some species have topknot feathers more than twice as long as the entire bird; others have two wirelike tail feathers. Some have broad plumes on the neck or broad tail feathers, which they fan out. They assume unusual positions in displaying their plumage; one even hangs upside down.

BOWERBIRDS (12–15 in.) are less colorful than the related Birds of Paradise. They eat mostly fruit but also seeds and insects. The males build elaborate bowers in which they court the females. Some add bright berries, shells, or other objects to the bowers and even bring fresh flowers, replacing them when they wilt. Some species build a bower as high as 8 ft. and use the same structure year after year. The 19 species live in damp forests of New Guinea and Australia.

REPTILES AND AMPHIBIANS

Reptiles and amphibians are cold-blooded animals—that is, their body temperature is almost the same as the temperature of their surroundings. Amphibians are the more primitive of the two groups, occupying an evolutionary position between fishes and reptiles. Typically, they spend a part of their lives developing in water and breathing through gills. Most adult amphibians live near water and have a moist skin. Reptiles have completed the transition to land. A dry skin covers their scales or plates, and they have lungs (some only one) and breathe air. Even those that live in water must come to the surface for air.

AMPHIBIANS are salamanders, newts, frogs, toads, and the primitive, wormlike caecilians. Salamanders and newts have long tails; adult frogs and toads do not. Amphibians have neither true claws nor scales. At mating time, even those that live on land return to water (or to a damp place) to lay eggs. The young, or tadpoles, do not resemble the adult.

REPTILES include snakes, lizards, turtles, crocodilians, and ·the nearly extinct and rarely exhibited Tuatara, or *Sphenodon*, of New Zealand. Snakes are typically legless, but a few kinds have vestiges of legs. Most reptiles lay rubbery-shelled eggs, but some give birth to live young. In either case, the young resemble the adults.

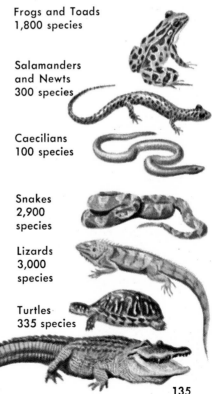

Frogs and Toads
1,800 species

Salamanders
and Newts
300 species

Caecilians
100 species

Snakes
2,900
species

Lizards
3,000
species

Turtles
335 species

Crocodilians
25 species

CROCODILIANS are long-snouted, long-tailed, four-legged reptiles with horny, platelike scales and numerous conical teeth. Found in or near water in tropical and subtropical regions, this group is divided into (1) crocodiles, (2) alligators and caimans, and (3) gavials. All use their tail for swimming. On land they lie flat on their belly, but they can lift themselves on their legs to walk—or can even run rapidly for short distances. Except when feeding, they spend most of their time sunning along the shore. In all crocodilians, the nostrils and eyes are on bumps on the top of the head, permitting the big reptiles to breathe and to see while the body (including all of the head except these bumps) is under the water. As "floating logs," they drift at the surface and catch their prey unaware. Captive alligators have lived for more than 50 years, slightly longer than any of the crocodiles.

American Alligator

American Crocodile

CROCODILES are the largest (not longest) of all living reptiles, some weighing more than a ton and reaching a length of more than 20 feet. American Crocodiles live in salt-water marshes and along brackish waterways from the southern tip of Florida to northern South America. The American Crocodile has a narrow, pointed snout; the American Alligator, a broad, rounded snout.

Crocodiles in Africa and Asia have rather broad snouts, but in all, the fourth lower tooth on each side still shows when the jaws are closed, distinguishing them from the alligators and also from the caimans. The False Gavial, of the Malayan Peninsula, has the most pointed snout of all the true crocodiles.

ALLIGATORS are found in only two places: The American Alligator (10–19 ft.) from the Carolinas southward and around the Gulf to Texas, and the smaller Chinese Alligator in the Yangtze River and its tributaries. Both live mainly in fresh water, sometimes in brackish. The related South American caimans—Black, Spectacled, and Smooth-fronted —are about the same size. In caimans and alligators, all upper teeth show when jaws are closed, but the fourth lower tooth on each side is hidden in a pit.

GAVIALS, of tropical southeastern Asia, reach a length of more than 20 feet, much longer than the False Gavial. They use their slim, garfish-like snout for catching fish, their main food.

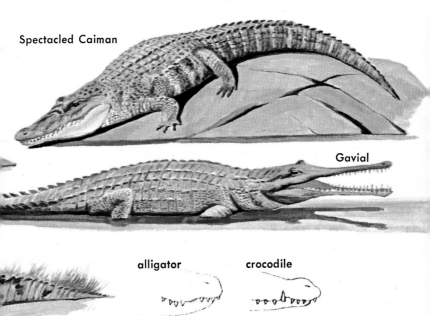

Spectacled Caiman

Gavial

alligator   crocodile

TURTLES, an ancient group dating to the days of the dinosaurs, live in such varied places as hot, dry deserts, swamps and marshes, open sea, and fresh-water streams, lakes, and ponds. Land turtles are mainly vegetarians; most aquatic turtles are flesh eaters. Turtles have an upper shell, or carapace, formed over the partially fused ribs, and a lower shell, or plastron. Turtles lack teeth, but the horny edges of their jaws are quite sharp. The largest of the turtles are the sea-dwelling Leatherbacks that may weigh up to 1,500 lbs. and measure about 9 ft. long. All turtles lay eggs in nests dug in sand or in loose soil, and the eggs are incubated by the earth's warmth. Turtles are longer-lived in captivity than are any other backboned animals. There is evidence that they may live for at least 150 years; some well-authenticated records exceed 80 years.

MATAMATAS, large, South American snake-necked turtles, have a short tail, 16-in. shell, a long neck, and a broad head covered with growths. Tubular nostrils serve as snorkels. When turtle opens its large mouth, fish or other animals are caught by inrush of water.

AUSTRALIAN SNAKE-NECKED TURTLES have a neck that is almost as long as their 6-in. shells. To hide their head, these turtles tuck it into the loose skin. The long neck is lashed out snakelike to capture food. These docile fresh-water turtles have lived for 35 years in zoos.

Matamata

Australian Snake-necked Turtle

Elegant Slider

Painted Turtle

SLIDERS (8–12 in.) are common North American aquatic turtles. Males use long fingernails to tap female's head in courtship. Commonly bask on rocks and logs. Young sliders are commonly sold in pet shops.

MUSK TURTLES, or Stinkpots, emit a strong, musky odor. These small (3–6 in.) turtles live in slow-moving streams and muddy ponds where they feed on small aquatic animals, living or dead.

DIAMOND-BACKED TERRAPINS (8 in.)—rings on shell suggest their names—live in salt marshes and tidal waters of Atlantic and Gulf coasts. They were once raised for their meat.

SOFT-SHELLED TURTLES (12–16 in.), of North America, Africa, and Southeast Asia, are flat and round. Their shells are imbedded in fleshy, rubbery material, like leather. Their snorkel-like snout hides strong jaws that can inflict a painful bite, and their neck is slim and snakelike.

PAINTED TURTLES (6–8 in.) are colorfully marked with red and yellow. Color varies with the region (Maine to Mexico). They often sun for hours on logs or rocks, dropping off into the water quickly when disturbed.

Stinkpot Musk Turtle

Diamond-backed Terrapin

ALLIGATOR SNAPPERS (24–30 in.) are the largest of the freshwater turtles, weighing up to more than 200 lbs. They live in the slow streams and swampy ponds of southeastern United States. A wormlike bit of flesh on turtle's tongue may entice fish to the opened mouth.

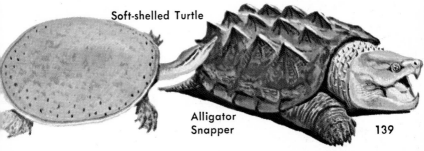

Soft-shelled Turtle

Alligator Snapper

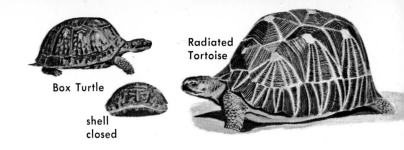

Radiated Tortoise

Box Turtle

shell closed

BOX TURTLES, if not too fat, can close their 5-in. hinged shells tightly. They do well in captivity and will eat fruit, meat, and insects. All but one of the several species of box turtles are land dwellers.

RADIATED TORTOISES, with a pattern of radiating yellow or orange bands on the carapace, are large (18 in.) dome-shelled, land-dwellers of Madagascar. Like other tortoises, they eat fruits and vegetables.

GIANT TORTOISES weigh as much as 500 lbs. Aldabra Giant Tortoises, from islands in the Indian Ocean near Madagascar, are common in zoos. The Giant Tortoises of the Galapagos Islands were so ruthlessly slaughtered for their meat, eggs, and oil that they were nearly exterminated. These giants are so docile that children are often permitted to ride them in zoos.

Aldabra Giant Tortoise

LIZARDS are typically long-bodied, scaly reptiles with movable eyelids, functional ear openings, and four well-developed limbs. A few kinds lack legs and resemble snakes or worms. Most lizards can shed their tail and grow a new one. The more than 3,000 species of lizards vary in size from 2 in. to 10 ft. and are found in warm regions throughout the world.

MONITORS are giant dragon-like lizards with a thick tail, powerful limbs, and an exceptionally long, forked tongue. Most monitors live near water and are excellent swimmers. The Komodo Dragon, found on several Indonesian islands, may reach length of 10 ft.; Nile Monitor of tropical Africa, 6 ft.

TEGUS are swift-footed South American lizards that may exceed 3 ft. in length and weigh up to 2 lbs. They eat small animals, fruit, and eggs. Unlike other ground lizards, Tegus climb trees and often lay eggs in termite nests. The smaller racerunners and whiptail lizards of the United States are closely related.

MEXICAN BEADED LIZARDS AND GILA MONSTERS (2 ft.) are the only venomous lizards in the world. Their scales are in "beaded" rows aligning crosswise and diagonally. Beaded Lizard, almost black, has more bands on its tail than the pinkish Gila Monster.

Gila Monster

Tegu

Komodo Dragon

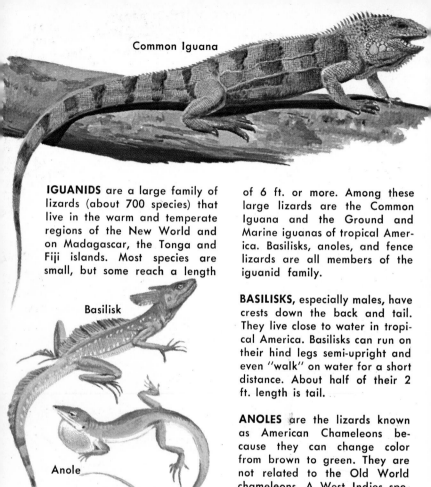

Common Iguana

Basilisk

Anole

Fence
Lizard

IGUANIDS are a large family of lizards (about 700 species) that live in the warm and temperate regions of the New World and on Madagascar, the Tonga and Fiji islands. Most species are small, but some reach a length of 6 ft. or more. Among these large lizards are the Common Iguana and the Ground and Marine iguanas of tropical America. Basilisks, anoles, and fence lizards are all members of the iguanid family.

BASILISKS, especially males, have crests down the back and tail. They live close to water in tropical America. Basilisks can run on their hind legs semi-upright and even "walk" on water for a short distance. About half of their 2 ft. length is tail.

ANOLES are the lizards known as American Chameleons because they can change color from brown to green. They are not related to the Old World chameleons. A West Indies species reaches a length of 18 in. Anoles are short-lived.

FENCE LIZARDS (6–10 in.), often called Swifts, are rough-scaled, swift-moving, insect-eating lizards of the U.S. and Mexico. Some males have patches of bright blue on the undersides. Most species are found in warm, dry areas. In captivity, they can be fed mealworms, flies, beetles, caterpillars, and grasshoppers.

TOKAY GECKOS (about 12 in. long) are natives of southeastern Asia and the Malayan Islands. They bark, giving a sound like "to-kay." Geckos hang onto the sides or tops of cages by means of microscopically small hooklike structures on the pads of their feet. They can even climb glass.

CHAMELEONS are slow-moving creatures. They wait for insects to come into view of their turret-like eyes, which swivel independently of each other. Tongue shoots out as much as 13 in. (twice the length of the lizard's body) to capture prey. Change of color is a reaction to heat, light, and emotion.

SLOW-WORMS are 18 in. snake-like, legless lizards of Europe and western Asia. In the wild they feed extensively on slugs; in captivity, they are fed insects and worms.

BLUE-TONGUED SKINKS are 2 ft. long ground dwellers with a broad, bluish tongue and a smooth skin. When approached, the tongue is extended and a hissing sound is made. Young are born alive. This Australian lizard does well in captivity.

STUMP-TAILED SKINKS have large, wrinkled scales and a stumpy tail. They eat insects, raw meat, fruit. Native to the warmer parts of Australia, they require heated quarters, as do other reptiles in cool climates. Over-all length is about 12 in.

Tokay Gecko

Slow-worm

Chameleon

Blue-tongued Skink

Stump-tailed Skink

Boa Constrictor

SNAKES are legless, long-bodied reptiles that lack both ear openings and eyelids. Some kill their prey by constricting it in one or several body coils. Others inject a venom that either kills or paralyzes. And some simply hold the animal down with loops of their body and swallow it alive. A snake's lower jaw can be swiveled freely at the back, and the two halves are connected in front by a stretchable ligament. This, plus the loosely joined bones in the skull, permits snakes to swallow animals several times larger around than themselves. The prey is held in the snake's mouth by the numerous teeth that curve backward. The snake moves its jaws backward first on one side and then the other to keep the prey moving downward. Snakes do not require large amounts of food and, in zoos, are usually fed only once a week. They do need water, and their cages are provided with stones or other rough objects on which they rub to loosen their skin and slide out to shed.

Reticulated Python

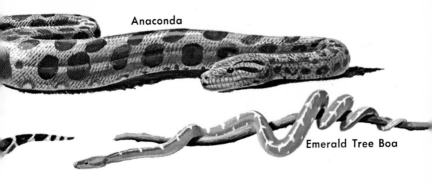

Anaconda

Emerald Tree Boa

ANACONDAS are probably the largest and heaviest of all the snakes. None over 25 ft. (about 250 lbs.) has been authenticated, but they have been reported to reach a length of 37 ft. These giant boas live in the swamps and rivers of tropical South America. They feed on birds and mammals and may eat more than 100 lbs. at a meal. They do not eat often, however.

BOA CONSTRICTORS, of Central and South American tropics, are the most familiar of the snakes that kill by constriction. They reach a length of about 12 ft. All of the boas give birth to their young.

EMERALD TREE BOAS, about 4 ft. long, are tree dwellers. They move from tree to tree without coming to the ground.

RETICULATED PYTHONS, of southeastern Asia, are the longest (authentic records to 33 ft.) of the true pythons. They can swallow animals as large as sheep. Unlike boas, they lay eggs, and the female coils around them to help with their incubation. In zoos the eggs are hatched in incubators. A large Reticulated Python may lay as many as 100 eggs.

ROCK PYTHONS live in the grasslands and forests of tropical Africa. If they are kept well fed in zoos, they are sluggish and docile. Both boas and pythons have the internal bony remnants of some parts of the hind legs. Particularly in males, "claws" may show at each side of the anus. Many individuals exceed 20 ft. in length; one reportedly over 30 ft.

Rock Python

King Cobra

Spectacled Cobra

POISONOUS SNAKES

KING COBRAS, natives of India and Malaysia, are the longest (to 18 ft., average 8–10 ft.) of all the venomous snakes. When disturbed and displaying their hood, they may raise their body about a third of its length off the ground. King Cobras are the only nest-building cobras. The nest has two chambers. The female lays eggs in the lower chamber, covers them with sticks and leaves, and then lies on top or near by on guard until they hatch. King Cobras feed mainly on other kinds of snakes. In zoos they are fed rats and mice.

SPECTACLED COBRAS, or Indian Cobras, are the kind used by snake charmers. Proportionate to their length (to 8 ft.), they have the largest hoods of all the cobras. The black marks on the hood form a shape like upside-down spectacles.

SPITTING COBRAS (6–8 ft. long) can eject their venom from the special openings in the front of their fangs. They aim for the eyes and are accurate up to 10 ft. The venom will cause blindness if not washed out immediately. Handlers wear special masks when working with these snakes. Newly captured spitting cobras may spit at spectators and spatter the glass cage front.

Spitting Cobra

hood not spread

mask   snake stick

Banded Krait

Black Mamba

Green Mamba

KRAITS (6–8 ft.) are found from southern China to Malaya and India. The attractive Banded Krait has a potent venom but rarely bites except at night when it may be accidentally disturbed. During the day, it usually rolls up tightly and does not attempt to defend itself even if kicked. In captivity, the several species of Kraits are quiet and inoffensive but seldom live long.

MAMBAS soon become adjusted to cage life but nevertheless do not live long in captivity. Several species of these agile, slender, long-bodied (to 14 ft.) snakes live in Africa. The Black Mamba is one of the most aggressive of the poisonous snakes and is greatly feared. The smaller tree-dwelling Green Mamba is less aggressive. Mambas eat birds and small mammals.

BOOMSLANGS (4–5 ft.) are rear-fanged snakes that live in the open country of Africa. Their venom is channeled into the bite through grooves in their upper rear teeth. Mangrove Snakes are also rear-fanged snakes often kept in zoos. These 6-ft. snakes live in the coastal areas of Malaysia and Indochina.

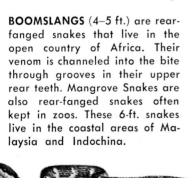

Boomslang

Mangrove Snake

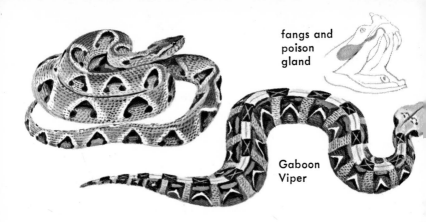

fangs and poison gland

Gaboon Viper

FER-DE-LANCES (6–8 ft.) named for their lance-shaped head, cause several thousand deaths annually in Central and South America. The fangs are long and sharp. They are primarily ground dwellers, give birth to young rather than lay eggs, and feed on birds and small mammals.

PUFF ADDERS (3–4 ft.) make wheezing and puffing sounds as they rapidly inhale and exhale air. They are found in the open country south of the Sahara and in Asia Minor. The venom is slow-acting but nevertheless deadly to humans.

GABOON VIPERS, bright-colored snakes of tropical Africa, may be extremely docile but their bite is dangerous. Their broad head is almost 4 in. wide, their body 6 in. in diameter and 6 ft. long. The back-curved, movable, needle-like front fangs are almost 2 in. long.

RUSSELL'S VIPERS, of the Indian Peninsula, are usually less than 6 ft. long. They prey on small mammals, frogs, sometimes birds. Active at night, they inflict deadly bites to bare-legged natives. Also called Jumping Vipers or Daboias.

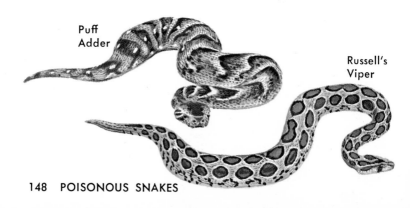

Puff Adder

Russell's Viper

Eastern Diamond-
back Rattlesnake

Timber
Rattlesnake

**EASTERN DIAMONDBACK RAT-
TLESNAKES** (to 8 ft.) usually
frighten off enemies by rattling.
The rattle gains a segment each
time the snake sheds, several
times a year. Eastern Diamond-
backs prefer dry, open land of
southeastern U.S. Western Dia-
mondbacks are slightly smaller.

COTTONMOUTHS, or Water Moc-
casins (4 ft.), do well in captivity and even reproduce. The
young are born alive. They have
no warning rattle. This southeastern U.S. species has a cottony
white lining in its mouth. It feeds
on fish and frogs.

TIMBER RATTLESNAKES (to 5 ft.)
have dark crossbands or chev-
rons across the back. Common
in wooded eastern U.S. The ap-
proximately 15 species of rattlesnakes in North America are all
poisonous to man. The bite may
be fatal if the victim is not treated at once.

COPPERHEADS (2–4 ft.) live in
the wooded uplands of eastern
U.S. and northern Mexico. Their
venom is less deadly to man
than that of rattlesnakes or cottonmouths. Their coppery color
looks like fallen brown leaves. In
winter they hibernate.

Copperhead

Cottonmouth

Indigo Snake

HARMLESS SNAKES

European Water Snake

African Egg-eating Snake

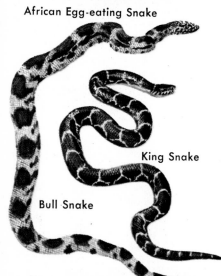

King Snake

Bull Snake

INDIGO SNAKES, of southern North America to northern South America, are among the largest (over 9 ft.) of the non-venomous snakes. Docile and readily tamed, their blue color is brightest just after they shed.

EUROPEAN WATER SNAKES (2–4 ft.), also called Grass Snakes, defend themselves by inflating their body and flattening their heads, then striking. They also emit a foul odor.

AFRICAN EGG-EATING SNAKES (1–2 ft.) can open their mouth wide enough to swallow large eggs, cracking the shell by sharp spines on the neck vertebrae. The shell is spit out.

BULL SNAKES, called Pine Snakes or Gopher Snakes, are light-colored with blotches of dark gray to black. Thick bodied and 5 ft. long, these North American snakes do well in captivity.

KING SNAKES (2–4 ft.) vary in color and pattern depending on the species. They kill prey by constriction and feed largely on other snakes (including venomous), lizards, and rodents.

Oriental Rat Snake

ORIENTAL RAT SNAKES prey mainly on birds and rodents in their native southeastern Asia and Malaya. In captivity they remain nervous and often refuse to eat. Some Oriental Rat Snakes are nearly 8 ft. long.

CORN SNAKES (2–4 ft.) are docile in captivity and feed on rats, mice, eggs, frogs, and young chicks. Found in fields and thickets and can climb trees. If disturbed, hiss and vibrate tail.

HOG-NOSED SNAKES (1–3 ft.) have a hard, turned-up snout. They are also called Puff Adders because they flatten their heads and hiss if threatened. If touched, they play dead.

ELEPHANT'S TRUNK SNAKES are 6 ft. long and heavy bodied. They live in brackish estuaries and in oceans of southeastern Asia. Females give birth to their young while in the water.

RACERS (3–5 ft.) are slender, swift-moving snakes of U.S. and Mexico. They live in dry, open places and eat mice, eggs, lizards, or other snakes. Racers vibrate tail rapidly if disturbed.

Corn Snake

Hog-nosed Snake

playing dead

Elephant's Trunk Snake

Black Racer

FROGS AND TOADS fold their hind legs tightly under them, making a springboard for jumping. Adults lack a tail or have only a very short tail.

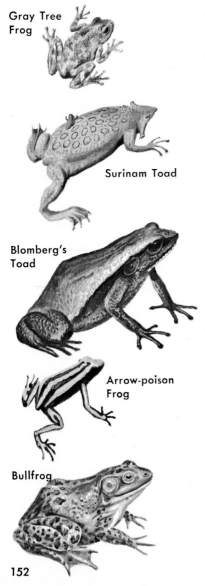

Gray Tree Frog

Surinam Toad

Blomberg's Toad

Arrow-poison Frog

Bullfrog

TREE FROGS of many different species live in trees and shrubs in or near water. Some can change color to match background. Feed on insects and make long jumps to catch them. Calls may be croaks, trills, or bleats. Most are 1–2 in.

SURINAM TOADS (5 in.), flat frogs with very broad feet, live in the Amazon and Orinoco river valleys of South America. When mating, a pair somersaults in the water, and the eggs drop on the female's back. They sink into the skin, develop, and hatch.

BLOMBERG'S TOADS measure nearly 9 in. and weigh several pounds. Their native habitat is the foothills of southwestern Colombia. These large, handsome toads are not timid, and they do well in captivity.

ARROW-POISON FROGS (2 in.) have a poison in their skin glands sufficiently strong to immobilize an animal as large as a monkey. Newly laid eggs are attached to male's back where young hatch and tadpoles grow.

BULLFROGS, the largest U.S. frogs, have a 4 to 6 in. body and long legs. Adult size is reached in 5 years. Bullfrogs live in swampy areas or in shallow lakes. The hind legs are considered a delicacy.

SALAMANDERS have a tail and their front and hind legs are nearly equal in size. All start life in water, but some are land-dwellers as adults.

GIANT SALAMANDERS, the largest of all living amphibians, reach a length of 5 ft. and are native to Japan; another kind to China. Entirely aquatic, they feed on fish, worms, rodents, and other salamanders. They must surface to breathe.

EUROPEAN SPOTTED SALA-MANDERS (4–6 in.) hide under damp logs or rocks and feed on snails and insects. They hibernate during winter. Skin can produce a poisonous excretion. Young possess gills; adults have lost them and leave the water.

AMPHIUMAS, known also as Conger-eels or Lamper Eels, are found in southeastern U.S. They have tiny, useless legs on a 3-ft. long, eel-like body. They live in drainage ditches and sloughs. Adults lack gills and must surface to breathe air.

MUDPUPPIES, or Water Dogs, live in lakes and streams of eastern U.S. and Canada. The bushy, red gills are retained and used throughout life. Hatchlings are about 1 in. long; adults, 12 in. A related southern Europe species lives in caves.

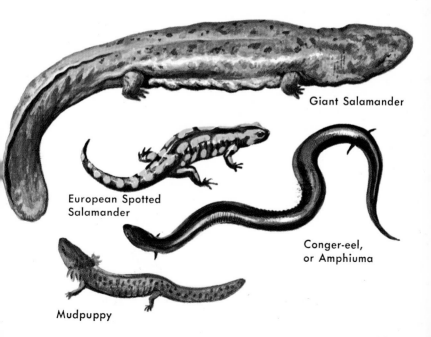

Giant Salamander

European Spotted Salamander

Conger-eel, or Amphiuma

Mudpuppy

NEAR-MAXIMUM AGES
FOR SOME ZOO ANIMALS

to 10 yrs.

Tarsier 3(12?)
Pigmy Marmoset 5
Tasmanian Devil 5
Mamba 5
Tree Shrew 6(?)
Pronghorn 8
Giant Panda 8+
Capybara 9
Potto 9
Rock Hyrax 9
Komodo Dragon
  9¼+

10 to 20 yrs.

Springbok 10
North American
  Beaver 10
Roseate Spoonbill
  10½
Dhole 11
Common Marmoset
  11½
Red Fox 12
Rock Wallaby 12
Spectacled Cobra
  12⅓
Silver Pheasant 13
Lesser Panda 13
Aardvark 13+
Platypus 14
Kookaburra 14
Giant Anteater 14⅓
Coatimundi 14¾
Monitors 15+
Muntjac 15
Agouti 15½
Aoudad 15½
White-tailed Gnu 16
Bullfrog 16
Wolf 16¼
Common Waterbuck
  16½
Weaver Bird 16½+
Red Kangaroo 17
Clouded Leopard 17
Mallard 17
Starling 17
Spider Monkey 18
Binturong 18
Gemsbok 18
Babirusa 19
Vicuña 19
Tiger 19½

20 to 30 yrs.

American Badger 20
Black Swan 20
Brown Capuchin 20½
California Sea Lion
  20½
Sun Bear 20½
Budgerigars 21—
Diamond-backed
  Terrapin 21+
Nilgai 21½
Drill 22+
Yak 22
Chamois 22
Reticulated Python 22
False Gavial 23
Two-toed Sloth 23
Peafowl 23
Boa Constrictor 23
Cockatiel 24
European Spotted
  Salamander 24
Green Guenon 24
Gila Monster 24½
Hamadryas Baboon
  24+
Snowy Owl 24½
Spotted Hyenas 25
Common Eland 25
Brown Lemur 25½
Wombat 26
Bactrian Camel 26
Bison 26
Caracara 26
King Penguin 26
Sarus Crane 26
Raven 26
Cape Buffalo 26⅓
Mandrill 26½
Amphiuma 27
Chacma Baboon 27½
Black Caiman 28
Moor Macaque 28
Baringo Giraffe 28
Herring Gull 28
Arabian Camel 28½
African Black
  Rhinoceros 28+
Rhesus Monkey 29
Lion 29
Onager 29
Anaconda 29
Sulfur-crested
  Cockatoo 29¼
Water Buffalo 29⅓
Brown Pelican 29½

30 to 40 yrs.

Lammergeyer 30
Scarlet Macaw 30⅔
Red and Blue Macaw
  30⅔
King Vulture 30+
Cassowary 31
White-handed Gibbon
  31½
Grizzly Bear 31½
Shoebill Stork 31+
Emu 32
Orangutan 32½
Coastal Gorilla 33½
Polar Bear 33⅓
Brown Bear 37
African Elephant 38
Pigmy Hippopotamus
  39½

40 to 50 yrs.

Chimpanzee 40
Indian Rhinoceros
  40+?
Giant Salamander
  40+
Alligator Snapper 42
Gold-and-blue Macaw
  43
European Flamingo
  44
Asian Elephant 48
Crowned Pigeon 49
White Pelican 49
Echidna 49½
Hippopotamus 49½
African Gray Parrot
  49⅔+

over 50 yrs.

Chinese Alligator
  50+
American Alligator
  56+

over 60 yrs.

Giant Tortoise
  31⅔+ (100?)
Aldabra Tortoise
  68 (100?)
Box Turtle 80+
Radiated Tortoise 85?

The scientific names of the species illustrated in this book are listed as nearly as possible in the order in which the animals appear on the designated page. Alternate generic or species names are in brackets.

14 Plat.: *Ornithorhynchus anatinus*
   Echid.: *Tachyglossus aculeatus*
15 Tasman.: *Sarcophilus harrisii*
   Wombat: *Vombatus hirsutus*
   Koala: *Phascolarctos cinereus*
16 Red: *Macropus rufus*
   Great Gray: M. *canguru major*
17 Brush-: *Petrogale penicillata*
   Ring-tailed: *P. xanthopus*
   Red-: *Wallabia rufogrisea*
18 Tree: *Dendrolagus matschiei*
   Wallaroo: *Osphranter robustus*
   Amer.: *Didelphis marsupialis*
   Mouse: *Marmosa mexicana*
19 *Gorilla gorilla*
20 Orangutan: *Pongo pygmaeus*
   White-handed: *Hylobates lar*
   Sia.: *Symphalangus syndactylus*
21 *Pan troglodytes*
22 Celebes: *Cynopithecus niger*
   Barbary: *Macaca sylvana*
23 Brown Stump.: M. *speciosa*
   Rhesus: M. *mulatta*
   Javan: M. *irus mordax*
   Pig-tailed: M. *nemestrina*
24 Mona: *Cercopithecus mona*
   De Brazza's: C. *neglectus*
   Diana: C. *diana*
   Green: C. *aethiops*
25 Mustached: C. *cephus*
   Spot-nosed: C. *nictitans*
   Patas: *Erythrocebus [C.] patas*
26 Javan: *Presbytis pyrrhus*
   Guereza: *Colobus polykomos*
27 Gray-: *Cercocebus albigena*
   White-: C. *torquatus torquatus*
   Sooty: C. *fuliginosus*
28 Chacma: *Papio ursinus*
   Gelada: *Theropithecus gelada*
   Hamadryas: *Papio hamadryas*
29 Drill: *Mandrillus leucophaeus*
   Mandrill: M. *sphinx*
30 Woolly: *Lagothrix pygmaea*
   Night: *Aotus trivirgatus*
31 Brown: *Cebus apella*
   Black-capped: C. *nigrivittatus*
   White-throated: C. *capucinus*
   Spider: *Ateles geoffroyi*
32 Squirrel: *Saimiri sciureus*
   Red: *Cacajao rubicundus*
   White: C. *calvus*
   Red Titi: *Callicebus cupreus*
   White-faced: *Pithecia pithecia*
33 Golden: *Leontocebus rosalia*
   Common: *Callithrix jacchus*
   Pigmy: *Cebuella pygmaea*

34 Tree Shrew: *Tupaia glis*
   Tarsier: *Tarsius spectrum*
   Potto: *Perodicticus potto*
   Galago: *Galago senegalensis*
35 Ring-tailed Lemur: *Lemur catta*
   Mongoose Lemur: L. *mongoz*
   Ruffed Lemur: L. *variegatus*
   Slow Loris: *Nycticebus coucang*
36 *Thalarctos maritimus*
37 Brown Bear: *Ursus arctos*
   Grizzly Bear: U. *horribilis*
38 Bl.: U. *[Euarctos] americanus*
   Sun: *Helarctos malayanus*
   Sloth: *Melursus ursinus*
39 Giant: *Ailuropoda melanoleuca*
   Lesser: *Ailurus fulgens*
40 Kinkajou: *Potos flavus*
   Coatimundi: *Nasua narica*
   Raccoon: *Procyon lotor*
   Hog-: *Conepatus mesoleucus*
   Striped: *Mephitis mephitis*
   Spotted: *Spilogale putorius*
41 Wolverine: *Gulo gulo*
   Tayra: *Eira [Tayra] barbara*
   Honey: *Mellivora capensis*
   Amazon: *Pteronura braziliensis*
   Amer. River: *Lutra canadensis*
42 Binturong: *Arctictis binturong*
   Palm Civet: *Paguma larvata*
   Mongoose: *Herpestes javanicus*
   Meerkat: *Suricata suricatta*
43 Spotted Hyena: *Crocuta crocuta*
   Striped Hyena: *Hyaena hyaena*
44 *Panthera [Felis] leo*
46 P. *[Felis] tigris*
47 Leopard: P. *[Felis] pardus*
   Snow Leopard: P. *[Felis] uncia*
   Clouded: P. *[Felis] nebulosa*
48 Jaguar: *Felis [Panthera] onca*
   Cheetah: *Acinonyx jubatus*
49 Cara.: *Felis [Caracal] caracal*
   Serval: F. *[Leptailurus] serval*
   Ocelot: F. *[Leopardus] pardalis*
   Golden Cat: F. *temminckii*
50 Lynx: *Lynx canadensis*
   Bobcat: L. *rufus*
   Mountain Lion: *Felis concolor*
   Jag.: F. *[Herpailurus] eyra*
51 Wolf: *Canis lupus*
   Dhole: *Cuon alpinus*
   Coyote: *Canis latrans*
   Yellow Jackal: C. *[Thos] aureus*
52 Red: *Vulpes vulpes*
   Gray: *Urocyon cinereoargenteus*
   Fennec: *Fennecus zerda*

Bow.: *Ptilonorhynchus
violaceus*
136 Allig.: *Alligator mississippiensis*
Crocodile: *Crocodylus acutus*
137 Spect.: *Caiman sclerops*
Gavial: *Gavialis gangeticus*
138 Snake-: *Emydura macquari*
Matamata: *Chelys fimbriata*
139 El.: *Pseudemys scripta elegans*
Painted: *Chrysemys picta*
Musk: *Sternotherus odoratus*
Terrapin: *Malaclemys terrapin*
Soft-shelled: *Trionyx spiniferus*
Allig.: *Macroclemys temmincki*
140 Box Turtle: *Terrapene carolina*
Radiated: *Testudo radiata*
Aldabra: *T. gigantea*
141 Gila: *Heloderma suspectum*
Teg.: *Tupinambis
nigropunctatus*
Komodo: *Varanus komodoensis*
142 Common: *Iguana iguana*
Basilisk: *Basiliscus plumifrons*
Anole: *Anolis stratulus*
Fence: *Sceloporus undulatus*
143 Tokay Gecko: *Gekko gecko*
Cham.: *Chamaeleo chamaeleon*
Slow-worm: *Anguis fragilis*
Blue-: *Tiliqua scincoides*
Stump-tailed: *T. rugosa*
144 Emerald Tree: *Boa canina*
Boa: *Constrictor constrictor*
Retic.: *Python reticulatus*
145 Anaconda: *Eunectes murinus*
Rock Python: *Python sebae*

146 King: *Ophiophagus hannah*
Spectacled: *Naja naja*
Spit.: *Hemachatus hemachatus*
147 Krait: *Bungarus fasciatus*
Black: *Dendroaspis polylepis*
Green: *D. angusticeps*
Mangrove: *Boiga dendrophila*
Boomslang: *Dispholidus typus*
148 Fer-de-lance: *Bothrops atrox*
Gaboon Viper: *Bitis gabonica*
Puff Adder: *B. arietans*
Russell's Viper: *Vipera russelli*
149 Eastern: *Crotalus adamanteus*
Timber: *C. horridus*
Cot.: *Ancistrodon piscivorus*
Copperhead: *A. contortrix*
150 Indigo: *Drymarchon corais*
Eur. Water: *Natrix natrix*
African Egg-: *Dasypeltis scaber*
Bull: *Pituophis melanoleucus*
King: *Lampropeltis getulus*
151 Oriental Rat: *Ptyas mucosus*
Corn Snake: *Elaphe guttata*
Hog-: *Heterodon platyrhinos*
Ele.: *Acrochordus javanicus*
Black Racer: *Coluber constrictor*
152 Gray Tree Frog: *Hyla versicolor*
Surinam Toad: *Pipa pipa*
Blomberg's: *Bufo blombergi*
Pois.: *Dendrobates trivittatus*
Bullfrog: *Rana catesbeiana*
153 Giant: *Megalobatrachus
japonicus*
Spot.: *Salamandra salamandra*
Conger-eel: *Amphiuma means*
Mud.: *Necturus maculosus*

INDEX

E